The Black Ceiling

HOW RACE STILL
MATTERS IN THE
ELITE WORKPLACE

The Black
Ceiling

Kevin Woodson

The University of Chicago Press
Chicago and London

The University of Chicago Press, Chicago 60637
The University of Chicago Press, Ltd., London
© 2023 by The University of Chicago
Published 2023
Printed in the United States of America

32 31 30 29 28 27 26 25 24 23   1 2 3 4 5

ISBN-13: 978-0-226-82872-5 (cloth)
ISBN-13: 978-0-226-82959-3 (e-book)
DOI: https://doi.org/10.7208/chicago/9780226829593.001.0001

Library of Congress Cataloging-in-Publication Data

Names: Woodson, Kevin, author.
Title: The black ceiling : how race still matters in the elite workplace /
    Kevin Woodson.
Description: Chicago : The University of Chicago Press, 2023. | Includes
    bibliographical references and index.
Identifiers: LCCN 2023006568 | ISBN 9780226828725 (cloth) |
    ISBN 9780226829593 (ebook)
Subjects: LCSH: African American professional employees—United
    States—Social conditions. | Racism in the workplace—United States. |
    Social isolation—United States. | Stigma (Social psychology)—United
    States. | Corporate culture—United States—Psychological aspects. |
    African American professional employees—United States—Attitudes. |
    Racism in the workplace—United States—Public opinion.
Classification: LCC HD8081.A65 W66 2023 | DDC 331.6/396073—dc23/
    eng/20230526
LC record available at https://lccn.loc.gov/2023006568

♾ This paper meets the requirements of ANSI/NISO Z39.48-1992
(Permanence of Paper).

Contents

Beyond Bias

After approximately four years at a top national law firm, Deborah's career was drawing to an unhappy close. She had reached a dead end. She sensed that she would never make partner at the firm; her senior colleagues were not providing her with the developmental opportunities and mentorship necessary to compete for partnership, and she had not distinguished herself among the other associates in her cohort. Even worse, Deborah did not have any promising options elsewhere, as she had not been able to amass the achievements or close connections with partners and clients critical for landing other competitive legal positions. Although Deborah still earned more than $3,000 per week and had not yet been passed over for any promotions, she was growing increasingly despondent about her situation. And because many law firms, like other elite professional services firms, use some version of "up-or-out" career models, in which junior professionals who are not promoted often are forced to leave,[1] she was running out of time to figure out her next move. Deborah left the firm shortly after our interview and within a few years had stopped practicing law altogether.

Deborah's career trajectory unfortunately is all too common for Black professionals working at large White firms. America's elite professional services firms—its preeminent law firms, investment banks, and management consultant firms—can be difficult workplaces for employees of all races. Between the long, sometimes stressful hours, the low odds of promotion, the often unrewarding work assignments, and the up-or-out personnel practices, most professionals who begin their careers in these institutions leave within a few years. But although careers in these firms can be challenging for all professionals of all races, they are especially difficult for Black professionals. Black professionals leave these firms more quickly and receive far fewer promotions than their White counterparts.[2] As a result, they remain highly underrepresented in senior positions. As of 2021, the partnerships at Cravath, Swaine & Moore LLP and Skadden, Arps, Slate, Meagher & Flom LLP—two of the most prestigious law firms in the country—were each only 2 percent Black, up from 0 and 1 percent, respectively, in 2019.[3] Other top law firms reported similarly disappointing numbers; some have no Black partners at all.[4] Firms in other industries do not share their diversity statistics as openly as law firms do, but the data available for those professions do not appear to be any more encouraging.[5] At Goldman Sachs, the nation's preeminent investment bank, only 3 percent of executives, senior officials, and managers were Black as of 2021.[6] Other banks, including Morgan Stanley (3 percent) and JPMorgan Chase (5 percent),[7] also reported low percentages of Black senior professionals.[8]

The difficulties facing Black professionals and the ongoing racial disparities at elite firms have been the subject of extensive coverage in scholarly and popular publications.[9] But in reflecting on her law firm career, Deborah offered a new perspective not captured in these works. While many writings on the tribulations of Black professionals have focused in particular on the possible contributing role of racial bias—the positive and negative assessments and feelings people have regarding racial groups and their members— Deborah made clear that she did *not* attribute her problems to racial bias.[10] Instead, Deborah described her difficulties as "more cultural than anything." She spoke of certain social and cultural dynamics within her firm that she believed posed unique challenges for her as a racial outsider. She found that the cultural norms at the firm seemed to revolve around certain experiences, values, and lifestyles most common among affluent White Americans. She explained, "The corporate culture itself is based on White shit—[I'm] just being honest. It is more class too, but it just happens to fall in line with Whiteness." She watched some of her White peers develop rapport with clients and influential colleagues with ease while she struggled to forge similar connections. She found engaging her senior colleagues in conversation difficult: her attempts to initiate small talk were generally awkward and unsuccessful, compounding her sense of alienation. She attributed these difficulties to differences between Black attorneys' personal backgrounds and cultural repertoires and those of their White colleagues and clients. With evident frustration, Deborah observed that "the powers that be" evaluated associates through implicitly "cultural" criteria that placed her at a disadvantage. "There's some part of the culture that I am not grasping," she explained. "There are tons of things that come easy to some people and don't come easy to me." These interpersonal difficulties tarnished her professional image. During a recent performance review she had learned that partners in her group questioned whether she was engaged in her work or interested in a long-term career at the firm, a perception that she attributed in part to her lack of interpersonal rapport with them.

Many other Black professionals hold views similar to Deborah's. They perceive that Black professionals working at elite firms face unfair hindrances and burdens, but they consider these disadvantages to be distinct from racial bias. Their reports of their career difficulties generally involve feelings of alienation, frustration, and isolation, rather than outright discrimination. These problems can be difficult to describe because the current terminology used to discuss race does not fully account for them. Related to race but distinct from racial bias, these disadvantages differ from anything professionals read about in college or professional school or learn about on the job in diversity training sessions.

These nuanced problems are a major source of Black disadvantage at elite firms, leading to a nearly impermeable "Black ceiling." This Black ceiling is the end result of a series of burdens, barriers, and obstacles that undermine Black professionals for the duration of their careers. Drawing evidence from detailed, life-history interviews with more than one hundred Black professionals who have worked in prestigious professional services firms, this book examines these challenges. In the chapters that follow, we will see the processes that give rise to the Black ceiling and the ways that conditions at even diversity-minded firms limit the careers of Black professionals.

Racial Discomfort: Social Alienation and Stigma Anxiety

The problems that I focus on in this book are varied and multi-faceted, but they share an important attribute. They all involve a social dynamic that I refer to as *racial discomfort*. Racial discomfort is the unease that Black professionals experience in White-dominated workplaces because of the isolation and institutional discrimination they encounter. It is a complicated phenomenon that occurs because of a combination of factors, including racial conditions in the broader American society, circumstances within individual firms, and the personal characteristics of individual professionals. It ultimately stems from long-standing patterns of racial stratification in this country, and it both reflects and contributes to the skewed racial demographics and power imbalances that are prevalent at elite firms. Through racial discomfort, race remains salient for members of underrepresented and stigmatized groups even in the absence of any direct manifestations of discrimination or racial animus. Because of the way elite firms work, everyday interactions, decisions, and social activities cumulatively can contribute to racial inequality—even independently of any acts of racial bias.[11]

In this book I introduce two types of racial discomfort, *social alienation* and *stigma anxiety*, that affect Black professionals in predominantly White workplaces (see the diagram below). Social alienation refers to the isolation and marginalization that many Black professionals experience because their backgrounds and cultural repertoires differ from those of their White colleagues. As I explain in chapter 1, professionals' careers at elite firms are dependent upon their relationships with colleagues. Professionals develop and solidify these relationships through informal interactions with each other both on the job and away from the office. As most professionals who work at these firms are White, these interactions often take place according to the cultural and social preferences of White professionals. And because people tend to gravitate toward and bond with others who share similar cultural and social tastes, interests, and experiences—a well-documented tendency known as cultural homophily—White professionals at these firms are better able to cultivate professionally beneficial relationships.[12] This process disadvantages many Black professionals. Because they have less in common with their White colleagues (for reasons that I explain in chapter 3), homophily limits their access to vital social capital and reinforces their feeling of not belonging.

I also call attention to another form of racial discomfort, stigma anxiety. Stigma anxiety refers to the uneasiness and trepidation that many Black professionals develop in situations where they recognize that they may be at risk of unfair treatment on the basis of race. At elite firms, their awareness of the constant possibility of prejudice can be a heavy burden. It causes many Black profes-

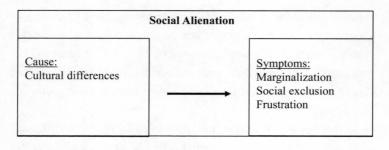

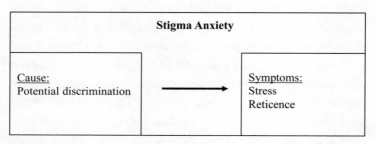

Types of racial discomfort

sionals to engage in processes that I refer to as *racial risk management,* in which they adopt self-protective behaviors to insulate themselves from possible mistreatment.[13] Although these reactions are understandable adaptations to fraught conditions within these firms, they can compound Black professionals' difficulties and further diminish their careers. Black professionals' responses to stigma anxiety, especially reticence and self-concealment, can reduce their access to opportunities and beneficial relationships and can even undermine their work performance. When Black professionals "put up a wall" by adopting defensive impression-management strategies in their interactions with colleagues, or when they opt not to assert themselves in ways that might advance their careers—such as by not speaking up during meetings or not pushing back against unreasonable work requests—they lessen their chances of succeeding. This is a lose-lose situation: though these adaptive tactics may help shield them from discrimination in the short term, they can compound Black professionals' problems over the long run. And of course stigma anxiety is psychologically and emotionally taxing. Having to navigate one's career while constantly worrying about encountering unfair treatment and other unpleasant experiences is highly stressful, and stress can undermine work performance and personal well-being.

Why Some Black Professionals Thrive: Explaining Intraracial Diversity

The concept of racial discomfort can help us understand differences in the experiences of similarly situated individual Black professionals. Social alienation and stigma anxiety affect some Black professionals far more than others, depending on their past experiences and present circumstances. Black professionals each have distinct personal traits, life histories, and resources. Therefore, there is no single "Black experience" at elite firms. Despite the long odds, some Black professionals manage to thrive, earning promotions and esteem from their colleagues. Thanks to the skills, connections, and credentials that they acquire in these jobs, they are able to advance within their firms or move on to highly sought-after positions elsewhere. Their very positive experiences complicate the conventional narratives, which at times present Black professionals as if they were universally disadvantaged, and underscore the idea that the impact of race is more varied and nuanced than previously understood.

Black professionals working alongside each other at the same firms often have very different career trajectories, and their views about the impact of race at their firms can be so divergent as to seem impossible to reconcile. For example, Sandra, a colleague of Deborah's, had a far more successful and satisfying career at their firm. In some respects, Sandra and Deborah seemed to be similarly situated at the start of their careers. The two women began working at the firm less than one year apart. Both had grown up in middle-class homes with parents who were schoolteachers. They both had attended prestigious private colleges. They had even graduated from the same law school. But despite these similarities, their experiences at the firm hardly could have been more different. Widely regarded as a rising star, Sandra enjoyed great relationships with several prominent partners. During our interview, she spoke confidently of her prospects of making partner and indeed was promoted to partner a few years after we spoke. Sandra explained that, to her surprise, race had not presented her with any serious difficulties or setbacks at the firm. When I asked Sandra how she felt about her time at the firm up to that point, she responded with unbridled enthusiasm. "Honestly, . . . I'll tell you I actually can't believe how many opportunities I've had," she insisted. "It does not get better than this. For me it's just been a very, very positive experience."

Sandra's description of life at her firm was not one of postracial bliss. Despite her own successes, she did not consider her firm to be racially fair. She made it clear that she believed Black professionals still faced unfair disadvantages, explaining, "I certainly don't want to come off as saying I think everything in law firms is fine, and if you work hard and pull yourself up by your bootstraps, you're going to make it. That's not what I'm saying at all." Sandra recognized that her views were not necessarily typical and that some other Black associates at her firm had opinions and experiences that diverged sharply from hers. She explained, "I really think you could talk to somebody [else], and they would tell you, 'It was terrible. It was racist. No, I didn't feel any type of mentorship at all.'" Reflecting on her own experiences though, Sandra emphasized, "I definitely don't feel that me being Black is a hindrance to me doing well at the firm. *At all.*"

Studies of Black workers often omit the kind of upbeat views shared by Sandra, but her outlook is actually not all that uncommon. Black Americans have long reported diverse beliefs about the significance of race in the workplace. In study after study and poll after poll, majorities of Black respondents have reported that they have *not* experienced racial discrimination at their current place of employment.[14] These views may be highly underrepresented in the existing literature in part because researchers are less interested in them and in part because people who feel this way may feel social pressure to keep their beliefs to themselves. Like other interviewees who were highly content at their firms, Sandra sensed that her views ran counter to expectations and had the potential to offend other Black professionals: "I actually found it difficult in the law firm setting where I know that I felt good about my opportunities, and sometimes it makes me feel more distant from some of the other Black associates. . . . [They] talk about how racist the firm is, how terrible the firm is. . . . I assume it's like being the Black Republican at Thanksgiving Dinner. I'll go to the diversity events and I try to give my perspective on certain things and I just notice that it's not always warmly received."

The divergence between Sandra's experiences and those of her colleagues speaks to the complex, highly varied nature of racial disadvantage in the modern workplace. It also raises a number of interesting questions. What are we to make of the diverse experiences and conflicting viewpoints of Black professionals working in the same firms? How do some Black professionals manage to thrive in these firms while others crash and burn? Why are some Black professionals more susceptible to and affected by racial discomfort than others? Do the variations in their career trajectories reflect differences in their personal backgrounds? Though previous research has provided important insights into certain aspects of Black professionals' experiences at White firms, these intraracial differences remain somewhat of a mystery.[15] Yet they are important: understanding why certain individuals thrive in professional services firms, receiving high-quality opportunities, support from colleagues, and promotions or elite positions elsewhere, offers new insights into the overall predicament of Black professionals. Therefore, to fully understand the experiences of Black professionals at elite firms and the nature of the opportunities and obstacles that they face there, we must closely consider those of people who, like Sandra, have thrived.

RACIAL SEPARATENESS AND WHITE FAMILIARITY

Evidence from my interviews suggests that Black professionals' prior life experiences affect how much racial discomfort they feel in White work settings. Specifically, their previous relationships and interactions with White people—or the lack thereof—can have a profound impact. Many Black professionals—including those who have attended predominantly White schools—hail from socially segregated backgrounds, having had relatively limited interracial social relationships and interactions during their university years and, in some instances, childhoods. For example, Deborah's difficulties at her firm likely stem in part from the fact that she experienced racial separateness throughout her childhood and in school. Deborah had grown up in a predominantly Black and Latino urban neighborhood and had very few White classmates throughout elementary school and junior high school. She attended a more diverse high school and a large, predominantly White institution (PWI) for college, but Deborah gravitated toward Black social circles and student organizations in those schools and spent very little time socializing in White spaces. Worse, Deborah had a number of uncomfortable run-ins with some of her White peers in college that further discouraged her from attempting to make cross-racial friendships.

Deborah's background is not at all uncommon. Although university marketing materials often depict scenes of racially diverse groups of friends, on college campuses Black and White students generally lead racially separate social lives.[16] As a result, many Black professionals begin their careers with surprisingly limited prior interracial relationships or immersion in their schools' White "mainstream" social settings. This racial separateness occurs for a variety of reasons, including students' homophily preferences, Black students' concerns about their White classmates' racial attitudes, and campus policies.[17] It is not necessarily detrimental for Black students—in fact, it enables some to find valuable social support in what otherwise might be very difficult and uncomfortable environments.[18] Nonetheless, this racial separateness can become a professional liability for those Black students who eventually pursue careers in predominantly White firms.[19]

By contrast, many of the Black professionals I interviewed who were more successful at their firms and more highly satisfied with their experiences had begun their careers with higher-quality interracial exposure and social relationships. While Deborah originally hailed from an urban neighborhood that had long been segregated by public policy and White flight,[20] Sandra had grown up in a predominantly White suburb, where nearly all of her close friends and classmates were White. These life circumstances gave her a sense of comfort and familiarity navigating White spaces as the only Black person present, traits that likely worked to her advantage at the firm. Other interviewees who reported positive experiences at their firms also stated that they had grown up attending White schools, where they had enjoyed high-quality interracial friendships; several had been voted class or student body president at their predominantly White high schools and colleges. Some of these interviewees had close White friends and remained immersed in majority-White social circles in college, professional school, and beyond.

I argue that Black professionals who begin their careers having enjoyed prior positive interracial experiences in these other White spaces may tend to fare better than other Black professionals at White firms. Their integrated personal backgrounds give them greater familiarity with the cultural milieu of these firms and a greater sense of ease in the conditions of racial isolation they inevitably encounter at White firms. As a result, they feel far less social alienation and stigma anxiety. This advantage can be quite subtle, and it certainly does not ensure professional success, but in institutions that are both White dominated and relationship oriented, it can impact Black professionals' careers decisively. Thus, Black professionals with this prior acclimation to White social and institutional spaces may actually have better prospects of thriving in these firms than the broad statistics would suggest.

A PATHWAY OF INSTITUTIONAL DISCRIMINATION

So are Black professionals like Deborah at fault for hitting the Black ceiling? Is their racial discomfort just a personal shortcoming for which they have only themselves to blame? In the face of counterexamples like Sandra, it is easy for observers (including some of the Black professionals whom I interviewed) to misconstrue situations like Deborah's this way. But Deborah's struggles are actually a manifestation of institutional discrimination: firms' implementation and toleration of policies and practices that unfairly disadvantage the members of particular groups.[21] Racial discomfort is a mechanism through which White organizational spaces reinforce and reproduce racial inequality. Although seemingly raceless, professional services firms are in fact distinctively White in ways that shape the everyday experiences and career trajectories of White and non-White workers alike.[22] Within these racialized organizations, personnel processes consistently perpetuate racial inequality; the concept of racial discomfort helps explain exactly how and why this happens.

Racial discomfort is the result of broad social structures and processes, including segregated neighborhoods and schools, and the continued prevalence of racial bias in America. It can work in conjunction with racial bias, but it can also have an impact separate and apart from it. Racial discomfort can function as what management professor Nancy DiTomaso has termed "racial inequality without racism," which occurs when racially disparate access to resources (including social capital) generates disparate outcomes independent of any racist motives.[23] Put differently, the conditions that subject Black professionals to racial discomfort can produce racial disparities even if their White colleagues do not actually mistreat them on the basis of race. For Black professionals to thrive, then, it is not enough for firms to simply be nondiscriminatory—they also must attend to these other subtle sources of disadvantage.

The theories that I present in this book offer new ways to think about racial inequality in contemporary American workplaces. Building upon insights from a number of fields—including cultural sociology, organizational studies, and social psychology—they reveal that the disadvantages of race are even more multifaceted than previously understood. My findings shed light on strategies to be pursued and pitfalls to be avoided by employers and other people interested in more inclusive workplaces. They also identify characteristics that render some Black workers especially vulnerable to racial discomfort and others that enable some Black workers to thrive despite these potential challenges.

This Study

THE SAMPLE

This study's sample consists of 110 Black corporate attorneys, management consultants, investment bankers, and professionals who have worked in other high-status positions in the financial industry.[24] This sample is one of the largest used in any qualitative study of high-status Black workers and includes workers from more than fifty firms in more than a dozen cities across the country. It features Black professionals who all began their professional careers during the twenty-first century, at the height of corporate diversity efforts. Their experiences help illuminate how exactly race still matters at elite firms and how we might expect it to matter in the future. Though the majority (75) of the professionals in my sample are attorneys, and their reflections account for most of those that are shared in this book, reports from other interviewees suggest that the perspectives and experiences of high-status Black professionals at elite firms are generally consistent across industries. That said, I attempt to note any pertinent industry-based differences.

THE INTERVIEWS

The interviews covered the full scope of my respondents' lives, from childhood through their college and professional school years to their experiences in the working world. Through this life-history-style interview approach, I was able to amass one of the richest bodies of qualitative data gathered on the lives and careers of elite Black workers to date. These interviews provided the contextual information necessary to situate interviewees' discussions of race at their firms within the broader arc of their life experiences and professional careers. The interviews varied in length, with most lasting between forty and ninety minutes. I conducted the vast majority by phone and ten of them in person.

ORGANIZATION OF THIS BOOK

In chapter 1, "Institutional Discrimination at Elite Firms," I explain how certain practices and conditions prevalent in elite firms give rise to racial disparities. I focus in particular on the role of discretionary, subjective, and informal personnel decisions regarding assignments and assessments. This chapter also calls attention to the impact of the relational dimensions of professional careers in these firms, particularly the importance of relationships with mentors, sponsors, and peers, in disadvantaging Black professionals relative to their White peers.

Chapter 2, "The Dangers of Dodging Discrimination," turns to the lived experiences of institutional discrimination for Black professionals and explains how their reasonable concerns about potential discrimination can lead them to engage in coping and defensive strategies that ultimately compound their disadvantages. It explains that workers who are especially conscious of the potential for discrimination may, for example, refrain from speaking up in meetings, asserting themselves when they believe that they have been treated unfairly, attending office-related social gatherings, or revealing their authentic personalities to and sharing information about their personal lives with their colleagues. Though understandable, all of these actions can limit their access to relationships and opportunities and lower their chances of impressing their senior colleagues and clients.

Chapter 3, "White Culture and Black Professionals," introduces a powerful and previously overlooked source of workplace inequality: social alienation. This chapter explains that many of the difficulties discussed by interviewees involved the social distance and certain cultural differences that often exist between Black and White professionals. Because of the racially skewed demographics of these firms, Black professionals are forced to adapt to and accommodate the taken-for-granted preferences of their White colleagues, and many find this difficult and unpleasant. This chapter also considers how these race-based cultural dynamics operate in conjunction with gender- and class-based variations to further alienate some Black women and Black professionals from lower socioeconomic backgrounds.

Chapter 4, "Why Some Black Professionals Thrive," provides an in-depth examination of a group of Black professionals who often go overlooked in discussions of race at elite workplaces: those who are highly satisfied with their professional experiences.[25] This chapter focuses primarily on the experiences and perspectives of interviewees who had attained the greatest objective indicators of success but also considers other professionals who spoke favorably about their experiences at their firms. To offer a partial explanation for their positive experiences, this chapter focuses in particular on the factors that enabled them to avoid or overcome racial discomfort.

The conclusion considers the implications of the preceding chapters for further efforts to understand and address racial inequality in elite professional services firms. It identifies steps that both firms and Black professionals can take to mitigate the impact of racial discomfort. It also considers how other groups of marginalized workers might suffer problems analogous to those of racial discomfort.

The difficulties of Black professionals at elite firms are no secret. Scholars and other commentators have studied and weighed in on these issues for decades; in response, firms have undertaken sustained efforts toward becoming more diverse, inclusive, and equitable. But Black professionals still consistently encounter a Black ceiling at these firms. More fully understanding the problem of racial discomfort will provide new insights into the challenges that continue to impede the careers of Black professionals and undermine firms' diversity, equity, and inclusion (DEI) efforts. And this greater awareness of the full set of problems facing Black professionals is a critical step toward the eventual elimination of the Black ceiling.

1

Institutional Discrimination at Elite Firms

Upon first impression, elite firms would seem to be relatively favorable work settings for Black professionals. These firms pride themselves on being meritocratic institutions and go to great lengths to recruit racially diverse cohorts of highly talented junior professionals.[1] Vying for business from sophisticated, diversity-minded clients in highly competitive fields, these firms have strong incentives to provide their professional employees with meaningful opportunities to develop their abilities and to treat them according to the quality of their performance. These conditions might make elite firms more promising workplaces than many others for Black employees, but as we will see, these firms are still racially inequitable and exclusionary in important respects.

Elite Firms as White Spaces

The first step in comprehending why these firms cause Black professionals to experience racial discomfort is to understand their racial character. Elite firms are not raceless organizations. Although people seldom refer to them as "White firms," they have demographic, symbolic, and cultural attributes that do indeed mark them as White spaces.[2] Just as businesses owned and led by Black people are commonly recognized as "Black businesses" or "Black-owned businesses," these firms are White firms. They are White in a symbolic sense in that most bear the names of White male founders and other prominent White male alumni—including, in some instances, segregationists and segregation sympathizers—who led them at a time when they did not hire Black professionals.[3] They also are demographically White. Large firms have achieved some racial diversity over the past half century, but their professional workforces remain predominantly White.[4] The senior ranks in particular are still overwhelmingly White. As of 2020 White attorneys accounted for 90 percent of all equity partners at the nation's largest law firms.[5] At Cravath, Swaine & Moore LLP and Skadden Arps Slate Meacher & Flom LLP, two of the most prestigious law firms in the country, 93 and 90 percent of partners, respectively, are White.[6] White professionals are also overrepresented in positions of power in other professional service industries. In 2021 Bain & Co., one of the most prestigious management consulting firms in the world, reported that 80 percent of its US leadership was White.[7] As the vast majority of junior professionals promoted to senior positions each year are also White, this racial skew may well continue indefinitely.

Because of their demographics, elite firms also take on a decidedly White social and cultural character. The cultural milieus at these firms heavily reflect the cultural preferences of White men.[8] Within and across elite firms, different departments—and different informal cliques within those departments—have different sets of cultural preferences. Some have "fratty" or "bro" cultural orientations, involving more raucous drinking outings and heavily gendered "guy talk."[9] Others have more of an urbane hipster ethos, and still others have "country club" cultures, involving boating, golf, and the activities and interests more stereotypically associated with wealth.[10] But despite these differences, the cultural milieus present at elite firms are alike in that they reflect the interests and preferences of particular White professionals and in many instances are not particularly attuned to those of Black professionals. As such, practices at these firms center and "normalize" certain aspects of White male professionals' experiences, and many Black professionals therefore must adapt to gain full inclusion.[11]

The Whiteness of these firms is easily taken for granted as unremarkable—especially by White people.[12] But it is highly conspicuous to many Black professionals. In these White spaces even seemingly innocuous everyday situations can take on racial dimensions that impede, exclude, and isolate Black professionals.[13] This heightens both the salience of racial stigma and the disadvantages of racial cultural differences. In these jobs, where talent and technical performance alone do not guarantee success and interpersonal relationships are critically important, this racial discomfort profoundly disadvantages many Black professionals.

Career Capital

To understand Black professionals' experiences, it is also important to contemplate how the organizational structure of elite firms informs their career aims and ambitions. Even more so than some people appreciate, these firms are intrinsically competitive workplaces. By design, very few professionals can rise from entry-level to equity-partnership-level positions.[14] Those who aspire to partnership-level positions must outperform and outcompete many other highly talented workers in what is essentially a zero-sum game with long odds of success. Professionals uninterested in long-term careers at their firms may face similar competitive pressures if they hope to pursue prestigious employment options outside of their firms.[15]

No matter their ultimate goals, most junior professionals aim to acquire career capital, resources that either signal professional success or improve their career prospects, as exemplified in the table. There are several types of career capital. In addition to the financial capital of their salaries and bonuses, professionals also seek to obtain human capital in the form of job-relevant skills and knowledge.[16] They also stand to benefit from developing social capital, consisting of relationships with colleagues and clients.[17] Reputational capital—their professional esteem among colleagues, clients, and other professionals—also plays a critical role in determining their career trajectories. Finally, cultural capital also functions as career capital in that having the right cultural knowledge and interests can greatly enhance one's professional experiences and outcomes.[18] The stakes of acquiring career capital are high: the difference between success and failure at these firms easily can amount to tens of millions of dollars in career earnings and disparate access to high-level opportunities in business and public service. Even subtle discrepancies in access to career capital can have severe consequences.

Many firms have implemented policies intended to give professionals fair access to career capital. Firms commonly use assignment procedures intended to provide junior professionals with work opportunities that will help them develop and demonstrate their abilities.[19] They also use rigorous procedures to assess professionals' work performances, and these assessments inform high-

Human Capital	Reputational Capital	Social Capital	Financial Capital	Cultural Capital
Work-relevant skills and experiences	Favorable performance evaluations Informal praise	Sponsors Mentors Workplace friendships Client relationships	Compensation (salaries and bonuses)	Knowledge and tastes concerning valued lifestyle traits (e.g., golf, *Seinfeld*)

stakes personnel decisions about compensation, promotions, and terminations. Many firms also use formal mentorship programs intended to give all junior professionals support and guidance. But although these policies promote greater equity, they have their limits. Specifically, firms still permit—and sometimes require— senior professionals to exercise discretion and subjectivity in allocating opportunities, resources, and rewards to their junior colleagues.[20] This inevitably leads to uneven treatment in countless everyday actions and decisions. As I explain in this chapter, these discrepancies consistently disadvantage Black professionals and thereby perpetuate racial inequality. As such, they are pathways of institutional discrimination.

All Assignments Aren't Equal

The divergence between successful and unsuccessful careers often begins with discrepancies in work assignments. At large firms assignments vary considerably in quality, and some provide far more career capital than others.[21] The most valuable generally entail either sophisticated substantive responsibilities or in-depth work for influential senior professionals and/or key clients.[22] By providing opportunities to acquire human capital and social capital, these assignments can greatly enrich the junior professionals who receive them. Kevon, an MBA who had previously worked at a preeminent management consulting firm, described the types of assignments that were especially valuable in his industry:

> Could be the responsibilities, the client, or the type of work. . . . A good assignment is working under the top partner in your office for a major client, or doing interesting work with the CEO. . . . Building the relationships with them can help you in the internal tournament at the firm. It positions you to eventually become a

rainmaker of sorts. Or a good assignment might be something
high-profile that gets you a lot of attention within the firm . . .
[s]omething that is going to be a foundation or a platform to make
partner, like gaining deep expertise in a functional area or in an
industry area.

As Kevon explained, premium assignments offer considerable
payoffs in reputational, social, and human capital. By contrast, he
shared that his own workload largely consisted of "not good" assignments, such as "one-off" tasks and work for low-revenue clients in minor industries, that offered no such benefits. The impact
of these differences in assignment quality can be subtle at first, but
premium assignments are so much more valuable than others that
even relatively modest discrepancies in access can snowball into
insurmountable deficits.

Several of the most successful professionals in my sample explained that receiving high-quality assignments early in their time
at their firms had been pivotal to their career trajectories. Rachel,
an associate who later made partner at her law firm, reported that
her performance on certain assignments led partners to regard her
as having "partner potential" early in her career. She explained that
these responsibilities, which at times included "managing 60 to
100 attorneys," many of whom were senior to her, enabled her to
outshine her peers. Similarly, Henry, an attorney, reported that he
was able to land a prestigious in-house counsel position for a major corporate client because of high-quality assignments he began
receiving as a junior associate at his former firm. Henry credited
his career arc to his good fortune in working for a partner who
entrusted him with high-level responsibilities usually reserved for
more senior attorneys: "He put me in charge of a team of 20 con-
tractors doing doc[ument] review, and then also I was running
the internal research bank, which included associates of my level
up to fifth year. . . . [He] put me in positions that no second-year

ever should have had, but to my benefit that's one of the reasons why I was able to get the job at [client]. Because I had some exposure in that organization, and they understood that I could handle myself." By enabling Henry to impress his future employer, these assignments altered the course of his career. And even if they had not led him to his new position, the valuable human, social, and reputational capital they provided could have helped his career in other ways. High-quality work opportunities like those Rachel and Henry received also have important psychological benefits. Being entrusted with these assignments conveys to professionals that they are in good standing at their firms and have the trust and respect of their senior colleagues. As a result, these assignments can increase their job satisfaction and professional self-esteem.

Unfortunately there is not enough high-quality work for everyone. Most junior professional work consists of what law professors David Wilkins and Mitu Gulati have referred to as "paper work": relatively thankless, often routine tasks that provide little career capital.[23] Interviewees disdainfully referred to some of these assignments as "grunt work," "scut work," or "shit work" and complained that "smart high school kids" and "trained monkeys" could handle them. Junior investment bankers, for example, often toil long hours as "paper pushers," assembling Excel spreadsheets and PowerPoint presentations or performing administrative tasks for which they are unlikely to receive recognition or to develop higher-level professional skills.[24] Law firm associates often perform essentially clerical and administrative tasks, such as reviewing materials to find typos and filling in pro forma legal documents.[25]

Some grunt work is unavoidable for junior professionals, but an excessive amount stunts their development and limits their careers.[26] Donna, a government attorney who previously had worked at a large law firm, discussed the precarious predicament of associates who do not receive high-value assignments early in their careers. She commented, "You find yourself a couple years down the road where you're technically a third-year associate but you don't have the skills that a third-year associate should have because you were just getting piled with work that wasn't really teaching you or advancing you." Donna explained how this reduced attorneys' career options, through no fault of their own: "At the end of the day if you leave somewhere after being there for several years, and you don't have the experience that someone's who's been there for several years should have, wherever you're [seeking employment], they're not going to say, 'Oh, we understand, someone probably strong-armed you and didn't allow you to do anything substantive'; they're going to be looking for someone who has that [experience]."

Junior professionals who are unable to develop sufficient human capital early in their careers can find it difficult to do so later on. Elizabeth, an attorney, noticed that the partners in her group preferred to give their high-level assignments to associates who already had experience handling similar responsibilities. This tendency effectively prevented associates who had not received quality assignments as junior associates from ever catching up to their more advanced classmates. Elizabeth explained that this put her in a very frustrating predicament: "It was one of those 'chicken and the egg' scenarios where they only really wanted to work with you if you had that experience. But how am I going to get that experience unless you work with me?"[27] When partners all act this way, their actions, in the aggregate, lock in any initial inequities. Discrepancies in access to premium opportunities, if left unchecked, beget even bigger disparities.

Recognizing this, some professionals quit their jobs and leave their firms if they do not receive sufficient high-quality opportunities. Megan, a federal prosecutor, explained that the low quality of her work assignments led her to leave her former law firm within two years of her start date. "They gave me assignments and projects to keep me busy, but at the end of the day I felt like I had nothing to show for it," she recalled. "I was working like 20-hour days on these crazy matters . . . and even with all the work that I did, I had nothing. I had no skill set." Distressed, Megan decided to leave her firm to salvage her career before she fell prohibitively behind in her professional development and could not pursue competitive positions elsewhere.

Although most firms have adopted formal assignment procedures wherein designated coordinators allocate work opportunities according to junior professionals' developmental needs, skills, and availability, senior professionals still maintain considerable latitude to staff their matters as they see fit.[28] Many routinely work around their firms' procedures by personally "grabbing" their preferred junior colleagues to work on their projects.[29] Kevon described observing this practice at his consulting firm: "Partners often build relationships with managers and associates, so when they find people they like, they often try to get them pulled onto their project, so sometimes they work outside of the official process. Sometimes a person will approach you directly and say, 'I like you and I want you on my project.' He'll tell the staffing person, 'go get one more associate because I already have one lined up.'"

Although these practices are often in tension with the firms' rules, they are common nonetheless. As Oscar, an attorney, explained, "Though law firms have formal ways to distribute assignments, the way that you're really going to get the assignment that you want to get is to know senior associates, to know partners." Hal, an attorney at a different firm, noted that this is especially true of the most influential partners, who "can just come in and cherry-pick whoever they want to work on their matters."

ASSIGNMENT DISPARITIES

Senior professionals appear to use their discretion in ways that consistently disadvantage Black professionals. My interviews revealed widespread perceptions that Black professionals receive worse assignments than their White counterparts; a number of my respondents spoke of observing stark discrepancies at their firms. Clara, an attorney, described how she became aware of glaring disparities at her firm: "We literally had meetings . . . where [the managing partner] would go around and ask people sometimes, 'What are you working on?,' and you could hear the lists. You could hear the difference in the type of work . . . with some of the White associates around the same year versus what the Black associates were working on. . . . [I]t was just totally different."

What Clara related amounts to task segregation, which occurs when a group of workers receive less desirable tasks than their coworkers with the same job title.[30] Through task segregation, workers who formally hold the same positions in practice end up performing functionally different roles. Task segregation is an important but underappreciated mechanism of institutional discrimination.[31] It perpetuates inequality within organizations by relegating workers from marginalized groups to worse tasks that reduce their prospects of advancement. It contributes to disparities in human capital: the accumulated experiences, knowledge, and skills that determine their future career prospects.[32] Task segregation inflicts psychological costs on disadvantaged workers and deprives them of opportunities to acquire career capital. Although it does not directly alter the material conditions of employment (e.g., by changing professionals' salaries or job titles), it has significant downstream effects on promotion, attrition, and workers' external career prospects.[33]

Clara linked this task segregation to the discriminatory actions of her senior colleagues in steering high-quality assignments to White attorneys, including a new White associate whose office was next to hers. She recalled that "[he] would get tons of work. He would just have so much work that he would have to turn down people all the time. . . . I would see people coming in and saying 'Hi, how are you? I've got this new case, do you want to be a part of it?' And when I saw new Black associates come in [start working at the firm] they didn't get that same kind of treatment."

In welcoming their most junior White colleagues to the firm by providing them with preferential access to work opportunities, senior White professionals can already set the stage for inequality in junior professionals' very first weeks on the job. Samantha, an attorney, described suffering from such practices firsthand. She explained that during her first month at her law firm partners gave a new White associate 180 hours of billable work, while only giving her 60. This gap grew over time, quickly creating a significant disparity in the two associates' skills: "I only billed 30 hours [the following month]. Now at this point, the discrepancy sets in. She's getting training, she's learning things, so that in July when they ask who can draft a promissory note, she'll be able to say 'yeah,' and I'll have to say that it would be my first time. So then there's a perception of one of us being more qualified than the other."

Samantha's account reveals just how quickly career-altering discrepancies can emerge. A mere two months after joining the firm, Samantha already had fallen significantly behind her peer. Although the two still held the same job title and took home the same pay, because the White associate had received far greater opportunities to develop human capital, Samantha had become objectively less qualified than her peer for future assignments. Thus, this type of assignment discrepancy can easily beget even wider gaps. As senior attorneys rationally could prefer to work with associates like Samantha's White colleague, who have already acquired valuable experience and skills, even nonbiased partners may seek them out for higher-level responsibilities while relegating less experienced associates like Samantha to more basic tasks. In this way, initial racial disparities can become self-reinforcing.

Assignment discrepancies can also inflict considerable psychological harm on Black professionals. Agnes, an attorney, experienced this early in her career when she noticed that a White male partner regularly gave a White male associate premium assignments while relegating her to lower-level tasks. This treatment was stressful and diminished her professional self-confidence. "Of course I harbored resentment for that," she said. "Psychologically it affected me. . . . You start feeling like I can't do it or whatever. They don't have faith in me. And it almost transferred into me going, 'Well, *can* I do this?'".

Agnes's self-account illustrates just how pernicious assignment disparities can be. By undermining Black professionals' self-confidence and feelings of goodwill toward their colleagues, assessment disparities can inflict debilitating second-order effects that further undermine their careers. To secure high-quality opportunities, professionals must instill confidence in their senior colleagues and clients. Doing so can be challenging under the best of circumstances, and it is especially difficult when a professional suffers self-doubt because of the actions of her senior colleague. And when Black professionals, like Agnes, become resentful over how they are treated, their senior colleagues may misinterpret their ensuing behavior as evidence of a professional deficiency (e.g., lack of collegiality) rather than as a reaction to institutional discrimination.

Even when Black professionals persevere and manage to overcome this discrimination, doing so can come at a heavy cost. Earl, a nonequity partner at a large law firm, explained that to catch up with White peers who had received better assignments and to compete with them for partnership, he needed to bill more than three thousand hours in some years.[34] Although he ultimately made (nonequity) partner, he considered the extraordinary effort it took to overcome this treatment highly unfair.

There's a ton of White lawyers around here who don't have to bill 3,000 hours to get those kinds of opportunities. But my perspective was, "I'm not them." There is nothing I can do about that. I can't become White. I can't change how [the partners] think; I can't make them treat me fairly. . . . So my decision was, "I'm going to figure out what I need to do to get this kind of opportunity out of them and I'm going to do it." And that's what I did. And if it meant they wanted to work me like a dog in exchange for a couple of good opportunities, then I worked like a dog and got the opportunities.

The extraordinary hours that Earl worked came with significant downsides. They put him at risk of burning out or making mistakes on his assignments and at one point even affected his physical health. In making partner, Earl achieved a measure of success that eludes the vast majority of law firm associates. But his ordeal illustrates that even when Black professionals manage to advance to senior positions, that does not necessarily mean they have been treated equitably.

Subjective Assessments

Senior professionals also exercise discretion in evaluating their junior colleagues' performance on assignments. Like many organizational employers, elite firms use periodic formal reviews to evaluate the performance of their employees. In these reviews senior professionals provide feedback on the junior colleagues with whom they have worked.[35] These evaluations consider many attributes, including attention to detail, writing and communication skills, analytical abilities, technical proficiencies, enthusiasm, collegiality, initiative, leadership, ability to work independently, and finesse in interacting with clients. Organizational scholars critique performance reviews for being inaccurate and unreliable, but they remain prevalent and highly consequential at elite firms.[36] Performance reviews shape subsequent personnel decisions. Strong reviews position workers for salary bonuses, premium opportunities, and promotions. Negative reviews can doom them to lower-quality assignments and more intense scrutiny and may even lead to their being terminated. Critical reviews also can be frustrating and demoralizing—particularly when they seem unfair—and can cause professionals to lose hope, lower their ambitions, and disengage from their work. Thus, negative evaluations can be harmful even when they do not directly lead to adverse personnel decisions.

Just as important is that senior professionals also communicate their assessments of their junior colleagues to each other via informal channels. These word-of-mouth reviews can be just as impactful as formal evaluations. When a senior professional praises a junior colleague's performance, other senior professionals may seek out the junior professional for additional high-level assignments. Similarly, when the word spreads that a particular junior professional is unreliable, her senior colleagues may entrust her with fewer assignments, regardless of her formal evaluations. Negative word-of-mouth reviews are hard to challenge, making them all the more damaging. Some professionals only find out about detrimental criticisms in subsequent formal performance evaluations well after word of their alleged shortcomings has spread and their reputations have been damaged.

Senior professionals do not always assess their junior colleagues' work performances accurately. In practice, conditions at large firms often require them to make impressionistic interpretations of their junior colleagues' performance based on imperfect information.[37] Professional services firms often use hierarchical, team-based structures, in which junior professionals work collaboratively on assignments or funnel their work product to midlevel professionals who in turn pass them along to senior professionals; these arrangements can make it difficult to identify individual workers' contributions, let alone evaluate them correctly. As Zeke, a former investment banker, explained, in many instances "it's really tough to quantify who's doing what, especially on the junior level." Freda, another investment banker, stated that because of the team-based structure of work in her industry, "it's really easy for it to not be a meritocracy." She noted that "when you're on an investment banking team where it is really team-oriented . . . it's not about you and the book you trade and the exact amount of profit that you made in a year, you . . . can't point to a number that says, 'I did X.'"

Other investment bankers agreed with Zeke and Freda. Several drew similar contrasts between performance reviews in investment banking and those of finance professionals working in sales and trading positions, where key performance outcomes can be measured quantitatively. Nathan, a law firm associate, contrasted performance assessments at his law firm—which he believed were marred by favoritism, bias, and personality clashes—with those of equity and debt trading, in which workers were evaluated according to their precise profit and loss figures. Nathan was well situated to make this comparison, as he had worked on Wall Street as a trader before attending law school. He shared his belief that the individualistic nature of the work and the availability of quantitative performance measures in trading, which he termed "the purest form of merit," led to fairer outcomes: "You stick your fingers into the fucking market and you make money. It's that simple. There's no room for bullshit. . . . I was literally making the trades. Handling millions of dollars, just doing the transactions *myself*. So there's nobody to get in the way and say 'Oh, well, [Nathan], you're not a good trader because you're Black.' 'Did you look at my fucking screen today? I just made three hundred grand. What the fuck did you do?'" Although even the quantitative performance indicators available in jobs like trading do not eliminate all subjectivity or completely prevent discrimination,[38] the observations of Nathan and other interviewees suggest that they may help.

By contrast, in law, investment banking, and consulting, supervisors have broad discretion in describing their evaluatees' performance. The difference between a good performance and an exemplary one, or between satisfactory and unacceptable performance, is often largely in the eye—and the pen—of the beholder. This subjectivity and discretion opens the door to discrepancies, for example in the disparate consequences that different junior professionals incur when they underperform on assignments. When a junior professional commits a gaffe, senior colleagues decide whether to treat it as a harmless anomaly or as evidence of a serious deficiency. Harold, a former law firm associate, explained how the "huge subjective element" of performance evaluations led to some associates receiving more leniency than others: "If [the partner] like[s] the [associate], [the partner might] think, 'Oh well, you know what, they must have been tired or maybe I didn't convey the job correctly or what I wanted them to do, or there must have been something else wrong with it.' But if you don't like the person, if you don't have that sort of relationship, [the associate] could very easily be written off as, 'This person doesn't know what they're doing, they don't have the skills or the capability to do this work.'"

This discretion enables senior professionals to assess some workers more generously than others, giving them decisive advantages over equally talented peers. Freda, the investment banker, explained that in investment banking reviews, "you can *totally* protect people, like a hundred percent." She described the broad discretion of bankers in deciding whether to emphasize or disregard particular aspects of their colleagues' performance. "It's . . . so easy to protect people—protecting them by not making their flaws apparent," she explained. "Associates can do it for analysts, MDs [managing directors] and VPs [vice presidents] can do it for their associates, and everyone can do that for each other." This protection can have profound career consequences. Junior professionals almost invariably fail to meet expectations on at least one assignment; those who can do so without harming their reputations or losing future access to quality assignments enjoy potentially decisive advantages over their peers.

The subjectivity of performance assessments also makes it difficult to dispute negative reviews. Chinelo, who left the practice of law after a short and frustrating career at a major firm, reported that certain inaccurate subjective criticisms about her work performance hastened her exodus. She recalled one instance in particular when the partner administering her annual performance review revealed that her colleagues had questioned her commitment to the firm: "He said to me 'there is a *perception* . . . that you are not dedicated to your work.' Now, [this] was a point to which I almost *lived* at the firm. I mean, I was always there. . . . So when they said that there was a 'perception'—what do you do with perceptions? The minute I heard that I thought, 'I'm sunk.'" Chinelo's frustration over this review compounded her growing dissatisfaction with her treatment at the firm and her despair concerning her long-term prospects there. She left the firm within months of receiving that review.

ASSESSMENT DISPARITIES

As Chinelo's account suggests, because of the subjectivity intrinsic to performance assessments, Black professionals have little assurance that senior professionals will evaluate their work fairly.[39] A number of interviewees perceived inconsistencies in how senior professionals assessed and reacted to Black and White professionals' performance. Kevon, the consultant, shared that some Black consultants who met his firm's objective performance metrics still received unfairly lukewarm reviews based on criticisms concerning intangible attributes: "What ends up happening . . . is that even though they try to make [the reviews] based on a bunch of specific metrics, a lot of it still ends up being subjective. Like, maybe you do great work and you have great skills, but if you have a different personality than them, they may say something on your review like, 'He's smart, and he's great, but he might not be a team player,' and junk like that. That's when you get a lot of people like me who get frustrated." Thus, even Black professionals who deliver impeccable work product are not assured stellar reviews.

The subjectivity of performance reviews opens the door to distortion based on racial stereotypes. Harold, the attorney who commented on the role of subjectivity in the performance review process at his law firm, complained that partners evaluated his work unfairly and used language that suggested they might harbor anti-Black racial biases. He explained, "For the first time in my life, I started running into criticisms or critiques about 'doesn't grasp concepts,' or whatever. And to me, that's always seemed coded because no matter what we're doing, it's just not that hard. . . . Especially when you see what everyone else is doing and they don't get the same sort of criticisms." Similarly, Natalie, a management consultant, noticed that Black colleagues at her former firm— including some with exceptionally strong technical backgrounds— received what she considered undeserved and inappropriate questions about their "analytical" abilities.

Interviewees found that their colleagues responded to the mistakes of Black professionals especially punitively, offering them less constructive feedback and fewer opportunities to resuscitate their reputations. Brad observed that senior attorneys at his law firm seemed to ostracize Black associates who made mistakes, effectively dooming them to failed careers. He reported that when Black attorneys underperformed on assignments, "No one really says, 'Hey, you screwed up this, here's how you do it right. Let's get it right next time.' It's more like, 'You screwed up on something, and I'm afraid of you screwing up again, so I'm just going to blackball you the rest of the time.' . . . I don't really see that with White associates." As Brad's statement reveals, inequitable treatment regarding work performance can occur through inaction on the part of senior colleagues rather than adverse acts. The discriminatory nature of non-acts such as the failure to provide Black professionals with coaching and high-quality opportunities is difficult to detect in isolation but becomes conspicuous when comparably underperforming White professionals consistently receive more support. Similarly, harsh sanctions against individual Black professionals for flawed performances may seem justifiable in isolation, but they are unjust if White professionals receive greater leniency when they make comparable mistakes. Kevon observed such a pattern at his firm, where he perceived that Black consultants who committed errors faced more dire repercussions than their White and Asian colleagues. He explained that "for the Black people, it was disproportionately bad. There were stories of people getting asked to leave after a year. Being surprised, being told that they were doing well, then they have one bad project and then all of a sudden, they're being asked to leave. . . . But then a lot of these other White kids and Indian kids who had people that had their back, would have two, three, four bad projects and people would make excuses for them. And they would still be treated like the best thing since sliced bread." Because of these stories and observations, Kevon concluded that "the playing field wasn't level—that there were certain people who were running downhill and me and other people who were running uphill."

Discretionary Relationships

In choosing to share career assistance and social support with select colleagues, professionals form new relationships that go beyond their formal work roles, becoming friends, mentors, and sponsors rather than mere coworkers. These relationships are based in part on professionals' feelings of personal rapport and affinity toward particular colleagues. Michael, a former investment banker, likened establishing mentorship and sponsorship relationships to "picking a girlfriend" and emphasized that "you both have to *like* each other." Quincy, an attorney, posited that the key to building connections was "being someone that they want to have a conversation with, being somebody that they wouldn't mind talking to outside of the [office]." Indeed, some of the most valuable workplace relationships are those that have blossomed into full-fledged friendships. This social capital provides professionals access to preferential treatment in the form of extra guidance, advocacy, and leniency. Through these advantages, it can place individual professionals on different career tracks than their peers.

SPONSORS

Sponsors, senior professionals who use their authority and influence to advance the careers of their protégés,[40] can help their junior colleagues immensely by providing them with quality assignments, advocacy, and other forms of support. It would be difficult to overstate the impact of sponsorship relationships on professionals' careers. Interviewees insisted that junior professionals needed relationships with sponsors, whom they also called "godfathers," "rabbis," and "champions," to have any hope of advancing in their firms. Donna, a former law firm associate, explained the importance of sponsors: "If you look at people who end up staying at firms, who end up being promoted to counsel or partner, they are noticeably people who someone saw potential in. . . . [B]eing a lawyer is not something you can just read and learn." As Donna noted, without such sponsorship support even high-performing junior professionals cannot advance at their firms. In workplaces with this type of career structure, which sociologists refer to as *sponsored mobility*, relationships with the right senior colleagues are an especially valuable form of career capital.[41] Virtually all of the most successful interviewees emphasized support they had received from influential sponsors as critical to their career trajectories.

Sponsorship relationships can pay off quite literally when senior professionals advocate for their protégés during the high-stakes meetings in which senior professionals hash out promotions, bonuses, and terminations. Harmony, a senior associate who went on to make (nonequity) partner at her law firm, shared that a well-positioned sponsor once helped her receive a bonus for which she was technically ineligible because she had fallen short of her firm's preestablished billable hours requirement. "Sometimes it is about who you have at the table talking on your behalf in the meetings," she explained. "I wasn't bonus-eligible. But because I had talked to the right people, and because I had the right people at the table, . . . they ended up giving me a bonus anyway." Other interviewees used similar language in describing the value of sponsors. Regina, a management consultant, believed that her relationships with senior White male sponsors helped her survive a round of heavy layoffs at her firm: "At the end of the day . . . you want to make sure you have people who will have a seat at the table, pounding their fist or sponsoring you." Without such advocacy, even highly capable professionals can fare poorly. As Regina explained, "You can be great at what you do, and you could do a good job but if nobody knows who you are, it doesn't get you anywhere. And it's not enough to be successful. So if you're just some African American associate and you're working hard but you're not really building relationships [and] no one knows who you are, you're kind of screwed."

Another attorney, Oscar, believed that he actually benefited from being Black at his firm, because it helped him build rapport with a Black partner who became a valuable sponsor: "[The firm] has a system with an associates committee comprised of partners and associates who work on reviews together, decide compensation, decide promotions, and things of that nature. Each office has liaisons. Our liaison happened to be an African American male . . . We became really good friends and I think he looked out for me. . . . There were mid-year reports, and he would call me into his office if he saw things that were out of whack or that I needed to do to impress other senior associates or partners. So that definitely helped."

Sponsorship's advantages often are zero-sum. Every premium opportunity a partner at a management consulting firm steers toward a particular protégé is an opportunity that a different junior professional otherwise would have received. And when a partner intervenes to protect a protégé during a departmental downsizing, another equally talented professional may be fired in her place. This zero-sum property of sponsorship can compound its impact—and therefore its potential inequitable effects on the careers of junior professionals.

ADVICE FROM FRIENDS

Professionals also benefit from other types of discretionary relationships. Colleagues who are not quite senior enough to serve as sponsors can still provide more junior professionals with valuable advice and guidance. Midlevel professionals can boost the careers of juniors by giving them valuable inside information and, in some instances, work opportunities, as well as emotional support and camaraderie.[42] Danielle, an attorney, listed some of the ways that relationships with midlevel associates can bolster the careers of junior associates: "If you're a first-year [associate], become friends with fourth- and fifth-years. Because they can give you work if they're swamped. . . . They know the lay of the land, so they can tell you how to find work, who to get work from, the office politics, so on and so forth. And you can ask them if they mind reviewing your work before you send it to partners."

For these reasons, office friendships may lead to superior work performance, greater job satisfaction, and longer organizational careers.[43] Sylvester, an investment banker, believed that support he received from a midlevel colleague and friend once saved his career. He recalled a difficult stretch during his second year at the bank when his senior colleagues began bombarding him with more work requests than he could handle. Though overwhelmed by the sheer volume of these assignments, which he worried might cause him to make costly mistakes, Sylvester worried that turning down additional requests would anger his senior colleagues and ruin his reputation. At his wit's end, he eventually sought the counsel of a fellow alumnus of his undergraduate institution, a historically Black college (HBCU).

> Luckily, I was able to have a conversation with this guy who was a year or two ahead of me: "Dude, I am totally overwhelmed, there's no way that I can finish all of this work." He said, "Are you telling them that you can't finish it?" I said, "Well, no, I can't do that, can I?" He said, "Dude, you totally have to do that or people will run you into the ground." That is just one of those frank conversations that I . . . needed to have or I would have totally killed myself. After that, I started telling people "no," . . . which ended up helping me in the long run.

Sylvester explained that this colleague and other friends at the bank—a group of HBCU alumni who were only slightly senior to him—often gave him advice that helped him flourish: "It was good to have them to call and say, 'So, what should I be doing now?' to get the real low down on what's going on and who I should be avoiding. Like when I was choosing what group I wanted to be a part of . . . I could get a really, really frank conversation with people where they'd tell me, 'You don't want to work there because this guy's an asshole' or 'this group has a tendency to churn through analysts,' et cetera."

There is no way to measure the value of this support, but is easy to see how it may have enhanced and extended Sylvester's career at the bank. Without it, Sylvester may have underperformed or burned out because he had been mismanaging his workload or run into any number of other problems. Instead, he was able to impress his senior colleagues and eventually received an early promotion to associate. His experience demonstrates that although they receive far less attention in scholarly and popular writings than mentorship and sponsorship relationships, workplace friendships can also shape careers.

ASSOCIATIONAL DISPARITIES

Although Sylvester and Oscar benefited from their friendships with more senior colleagues, many other Black professionals are not so fortunate. Black workers suffer relationship deficits across a wide variety of employment settings, and elite firms are no exception.[44] Senior professionals exercise great discretion in deciding whether to mentor or sponsor junior colleagues, and interviewees perceived that this disadvantaged Black professionals. Brad, the attorney who observed that partners in his group did not provide constructive feedback to Black associates when they made mistakes, reported that they also seemed to ignore Black associates who performed well. "It's difficult to find mentors," he explained. "I see [Black] people who are actually really thorough with their work, and no one really cares to extend themselves. And that's something I don't really see with White associates. When they're good, people take note and start training them to be even better."

Kevon, the consultant, explained that White male partners who formed an "old boys' club" network at his office (twenty-five of his office's thirty partners were White men) began lavishing preferential treatment upon several new White consultants almost as soon as they joined the firm: "[My] incoming class was maybe thirty-four associates, and, from the start, there was a group of about maybe five or six guys that the partners immediately embraced. . . . The partners made sure that they were pulled onto all the plum projects. . . . They were asked to take leadership roles in the office in different random things; they were always pushed to the forefront. . . . It was blatant. Because these guys would be getting on great projects with the great people. The rest of us would be thrown on random stuff." Other interviewees described observing similar patterns, in which coteries consisting mainly of White males gave each other preferential access to career capital.

Those Black professionals who are able to develop relationships with senior colleagues often find that their sponsors have less power and influence than those of their White peers. Lionel, formerly a senior associate at a prestigious New York law firm, recalled a "very clear distinction" between the partners who sponsored minority associates and those who sponsored their White counterparts. While the White associates worked with a variety of partners, including the group's top business generators, non-White associates were generally relegated to working with less senior partners who had less clout and fewer resources. "The partners that I and my friends were getting aligned with were all the same," Lionel explained. "[They] were not the senior partners, not the top billing partners." These minority attorneys' relationships were still advantageous, but less so than those of their White colleagues. As a result, Lionel and the other minority associates received lower-quality and less-varied work opportunities. Although these differences are subtle, their long-term impact can be profound. While attorneys in Lionel's predicament can sometimes survive at their firms for several years without the support of powerful sponsors, they will not be able to compete for partnership or prestigious jobs elsewhere.

Interviewees noted that racial disparities in workplace relationships worked hand in hand with racialized social patterns away from the office. Several interviewees spoke of feeling socially isolated at their firms, and they contrasted their experiences with those of White counterparts who had developed close relationships with senior White colleagues. Clara, an attorney, described such a pattern at her former firm, which she referred to as an "old boys' network" of White attorneys: "You literally would see some of them hanging out with the partners in their spare time, or going out for drinks after work, and I'd never be invited to those kind of things. It just didn't happen. . . . You just would see them somewhere if you'd go to lunch and you'd just see the partners with one of the associates or a couple of the associates. And they would be male associates and occasionally the White female associates too."

Such social patterns can exacerbate workplace inequality. They enable the predominantly White in-group members to solidify their rapport and deepen their relationships with senior colleagues, potentially leading to better assignments, more generous performance reviews, and more advice and advocacy. These advantages can give them a decisive competitive edge over the many Black professionals who lack workplace relationships. Langston, a midlevel associate at a large law firm, explained that social closure among certain White attorneys in his department appeared to influence important personnel decisions. He said that in his group "the ability to get work, or to get good work, for the most part, relies on your being able to infiltrate a clique of people, and that's tough." Langston described the members of this clique as being socially close and demographically similar to one another: "They're White, they're male, they're typically married. . . . Their wives all hang out with each other." He explained that this tight-knit faction "took care of" each other to the direct disadvantage of the group's Black attorneys. He recalled an incident in which senior members of this coterie stripped a Black senior associate of her responsibilities managing a high-profile matter to "hook up" a more junior White male attorney who was part of their clique. In shunting her aside to boost their protégé, the partners deprived her of an opportunity to acquire valuable experience, enhance her reputation, and deepen her relationship with the client. This act alarmed and demoralized the rest of the department's non-White attorneys; Langston left the firm within months of our interview.

The favoritism that Langston, Lionel, and other interviewees observed is a form of opportunity hoarding, which occurs when the people who control the flow of resources in an institution share them with fellow in-group members while excluding outsiders.[45] Whatever their motives, when White male senior professionals selectively provide White male protégés with preferential access to human and reputational capital in this manner, their actions produce institutional discrimination and perpetuate racial and gender inequality.

This institutional discrimination culminates in racial patterns in attrition and job loss. Regina, a consultant, believed that such disparities led to a disproportionate number of her Black colleagues being laid off at her firm. She explained that in her view, "it's not about race—it comes down to your network, and it comes down to the fact that you didn't build one. . . . It's not like 'you're Black, and we don't want you here.'" Although the distinction Regina draws between race and relational capital is overstated—racial differences in social capital within these firms reflect long-standing patterns of institutional discrimination—she is right that relationship disparities can lead to inequitable layoff outcomes even if senior professionals' termination decisions are not racially motivated. The social capital gap also may induce Black professionals to "self-eliminate" by leaving their firms voluntarily. Kevon reported that his senior colleagues' refusal to give him the same interpersonal warmth and support they provided to some of his White peers influenced his decision to leave his firm for a position at a newer, smaller company. He explained, "I just felt that I was giving myself to this company and they weren't looking out for me. I just felt like no one cared." Careers at these firms are difficult even in the best of circumstances; being socially excluded and treated like an outsider can make them unbearable.

Conclusion

Notwithstanding the many rules and procedures that elite firms have implemented to systematize personnel decisions, junior professionals' careers are still shaped by the discretionary acts and decisions of their colleagues. These conditions set the stage for patterns of institutional discrimination in which Black professionals consistently receive less access to valuable career capital via fewer and lower-quality work opportunities; more critical performance assessments that undermine their reputational capital; and less social capital in the form of sponsorship, mentorship, and friendships. These discrepancies typically involve seemingly minor actions, decisions, and omissions rather than any one decisive discriminatory blow, but they systemically perpetuate racial inequality within these firms nonetheless.[46]

Although it has long been well known that racial disparities exist at these firms, their causes remain poorly understood. Racial bias—the leading culprit—contributes to these problems, but it does not explain them entirely. Other problems involving racial discomfort also pose substantial burdens and obstacles for Black professionals. In the following chapters I discuss two forms of racial discomfort, social alienation and stigma anxiety, that both can limit the careers of Black professionals decisively, even separate and apart from any acts of racial bias.

2

The Dangers of Dodging Discrimination

Many Black professionals working at elite firms worry that their colleagues might treat them unfairly on the basis of race. These concerns lead them to engage in a sort of racial risk management in which they constantly attempt to identify and then circumvent potential threats of discrimination. In doing so, they utilize a variety of coping and defensive mechanisms.[1] Some refrain from speaking in meetings out of fear that their words might draw unfair and unwelcome scrutiny. Others consciously avoid sharing certain personal information during their informal encounters with White colleagues to try to avoid revealing details that might further call attention to their Blackness. Some Black professionals who worry about not being seen as respectable act and speak in a style of formal restraint during interactions with White colleagues so as to avoid giving their colleagues reasons to question their professionalism and judgment.

These efforts help Black professionals mitigate certain risks, but they can come with a heavy price: attempts to avoid discrimination can be counterproductive and self-limiting, as they frequently entail considerable drawbacks.[2] They impede Black professionals from developing career capital and conveying key attributes that are valued at their firms. Further, these adaptive responses may be misinterpreted as personal failings or professional deficiencies of individual Black professionals rather than as reactions to legitimate situational concerns. For these reasons, Black professionals' attempts to manage the risk of discrimination can lead to outcomes just as bad as those they seek to avoid. Put differently, rather than countering racial disadvantage, these efforts may actually compound it. In this way, conditions within these firms can beget racial disparities indirectly, even without acts of racial bias.

Stigma Anxiety

Black professionals engage in this racial risk management because of stigma anxiety, the unease that people with devalued traits—such as Black racial identity—feel about the possibility that others will treat them unfairly. Stigma involves what Erving Goffman has described as "spoiled" social identities, traits that mark the people who carry them as inferior in the eyes of others and therefore unworthy of equal treatment and respect.[3] Stigma once referred specifically to physical markings, such as the tattoos that ancient Greeks used to mark the faces of slaves and criminals,[4] but it now extends to a broader range of characteristics and conditions, including mental illness, low socioeconomic status, homosexuality, and gender dysphoria. Its defining feature is that it subjects stigmatized individuals to stigma-based disapproval and mistreatment.[5] Stigmatized people suffer from negative stereotypes and prejudices that can result in other people subjecting them to various forms of discrimination, ranging from avoidance to abuse.[6]

In America, race is a source of particularly intense stigma. Black phenotypical traits and other markers of Black racial identity have long been subject to negative stereotypes and prejudices.[7] Black Americans are presumed to be lazier, less trustworthy, less competent, and less intelligent than people from other racial groups,[8] and these biases can subject them to discrimination and mistreatment in all realms of life, including employment.[9] Accordingly, many Black Americans experience stigma anxiety and therefore devote considerable mental resources to identifying, and protecting themselves from, potential discrimination.

People experience stigma anxiety when situational conditions make the threat of stigma-based mistreatment seem especially likely.[10] It is akin to stereotype threat, the phenomenon in which members of stigmatized groups underperform on certain tests because their subconscious anxieties about group stereotypes diminish their memory capacity and concentration.[11] But whereas stereotype threat affects people cognitively, stigma anxiety affects them socially, by leading them to perceive that interactions with non–group members are likely to be difficult, unpleasant, or even detrimental.[12] Accordingly, members of stigmatized groups adopt self-protective tactics, including some that have unintended consequences that compound their disadvantages. At elite firms, stigma anxiety has three effects in particular that disadvantage Black professionals: *racial stress*, the psychological burden of constant vigilance against mistreatment; *racial reticence*, a phenomenon in which Black people choose not to speak up or out because they worry that colleagues will assess them according to anti-Black stereotypes; and *self-concealment*, in which Black professionals opt not to share personal details that they believe might increase the salience of their racial identity and discredit them in the eyes of their colleagues. Each of these aspects of stigma anxiety pose significant disadvantages for Black professionals working at White firms, undermining their emotional well-being and limiting their access to career capital.

Why Elite Firms Trigger Stigma Anxiety

Individual Black people feel more stigma anxiety in settings where situational cues and information suggest that they are likely to encounter discrimination.[13] Although direct evidence of bias and discrimination is relatively rare at elite firms, other conditions convey to Black professionals that they should not expect to be treated fairly there. The difficulties of Black professionals at these firms are no secret; racial disparities and allegations of discrimination have been widely publicized in voluminous newspaper stories, memoirs, and lawsuits.[14] Empirical studies also have highlighted that some Black professionals perceive racial bias to be prevalent at their firms.[15] Critical race theorists have described these institutions as arenas of racial subjugation, where White people act to preserve White power and privilege.[16] More broadly, sociological research has found that workers from marginalized groups may be especially likely to suffer discrimination in employment contexts where they are highly underrepresented.[17]

Against this backdrop, many Black professionals begin their careers already apprehensive about the discrimination that might await them. Brad, an attorney, explained that many Black law students adjust their aspirations accordingly, even before they have begun working at their firms: "I think the cat's fully out of the bag now [such] that any Black associate going to a big New York firm knows the score. . . . It's like every Black lawyer I know has an exit plan from their third year in law school. . . . Like *no* one when I was in law school was like, 'yeah, I'm gonna go there and try to be a partner.' *No* one."

EGREGIOUS DISPARITIES

The hopelessness that Brad described stems from long-standing racial disparities in promotions and attrition at elite firms. Brad explained why Black professionals sense that their careers will be limited by discrimination even before they actually experience any unfair treatment by positing that "looking up and seeing that people who look like you don't get to the top of the mountain" conveys to Black junior professionals that they will not receive fair opportunities to advance. Lionel reported that his former law firm had not named a single new Black partner in the decade since he began his career there, and he regarded this pattern as clear evidence of racial unfairness. He posited, "There has to be something nefarious happening at firms that explains how you start off in successive years with classes of 10 to 15 Black lawyers and yet still only end up with one Black partner for an *extended* time." While few junior professionals of any race make partner at their firms, the consistent, near complete failure of these firms to promote any Black associates to partner alerts Black associates that their career prospects may be limited.

SELECTIVE PUNITIVENESS

Many Black professionals perceive that these disparities are the result of racial discrepancies in how professionals' work performance is assessed. They recognize that racial biases can lead senior professionals to assume that Black professionals are less competent than their peers and therefore more likely to make mistakes on assignments.[18] Such presumptions, in conjunction with confirmation bias—the tendency to notice information consistent with one's prior beliefs while discounting evidence inconsistent with them—make senior professionals more likely both to notice their Black colleagues' mistakes and to interpret them as evidence of incompetence.[19] This possibility is a major source of stigma anxiety for many Black professionals. A number of interviewees worried that their senior colleagues might assess their work performance unfairly and subject them to excessive punitiveness for any perceived shortcomings.

These fears are not unfounded speculation or paranoia. Some interviewees had trusted colleagues and mentors inform them that they were at risk of discriminatory punitiveness. Humphrey, an attorney, explained that his mentor, a White partner, once informed him that he likely would be held to a higher standard than his White peers: "There was even a White male partner who relayed to me that there are White [associates] who had more margin for error because the comfort level was there for inappropriate reasons. The partner told me, 'I don't agree with it, I'm just going to tell you how it is. There's no question—you can't fuck up.'" Although this type of advice may help some Black professionals by impressing upon them the importance of avoiding mistakes, by leading them to perceive greater stakes for committing errors it can also exacerbate stigma anxiety.

Other interviewees came to perceive the risk of unfair work assessments as a result of incidents they observed or learned about involving Black colleagues. Some spoke of seeing or hearing about Black professionals being precipitously "written off" for fairly minor errors while their White peers received greater leniency. Their accounts raise an important point concerning stigma anxiety: discrimination not only harms its direct victims; it also affects other Black professionals, increasing their stigma anxiety and causing them to recalibrate their perceptions about the fairness of their firms.

These concerns are bolstered by evidence from a well-known study in which the diversity consulting firm Nextions enlisted fifty-three law firm partners to read copies of a legal memo that had allegedly been written by a third-year attorney.[20] All participants read identical copies of the same memo, but twenty-nine of the partners were informed that the memo had been written by a White attorney, and the rest were told that the memo's author was Black. The partners who thought they were reviewing a Black attorney's work product identified significantly more mistakes in the memo and gave it a much lower score than the partners who thought that the memo had been written by a White attorney, rating it 3.2 out of 5 compared to 4.1 out of 5.[21] These findings confirm Black professionals' apprehensions that some senior professionals may be predisposed to evaluate the work performance of Black professionals more critically.

Therefore, Black professionals have reason to worry that their colleagues may subject their work to more exacting scrutiny and regard even minor mistakes as proof that they are unable to meet the demands of their jobs. This possibility of catastrophic consequences for even understandable missteps can lead even the most confident Black professionals to experience stigma anxiety.

Impact on Black Professional Careers

Stigma anxiety is not always completely detrimental. In some instances, remaining alert to potential discrimination may help Black professionals avoid mistreatment by informing how they approach their interactions with biased colleagues. But predicting and managing discrimination is not easy. Discrimination at these firms tends to be subtle and covert rather than blatant, so the evidence of potential unfair treatment is at best highly circumstantial. White professionals usually hold their biases surreptitiously (and many may not even be aware of their own biases), so it can be impossible for Black professionals to know who is likely to treat them unfairly.[22] Thus, Black professionals often must draw inferences from highly ambiguous information. In doing so, it is easy for them to reach inaccurate conclusions.

It is also difficult for Black professionals to know how best to respond to potential discrimination. Deciding whether and how to act to avoid or address discrimination is a complicated process that requires Black professionals to consider the possible benefits and costs of various strategies. And there is no way to know for sure whether any one course of action will lead to better outcomes than others. This racial risk management is tricky, and it puts Black professionals in precarious positions. Overestimating the risk of discrimination or underestimating the costs of a particular adaptive response can lead Black professionals to react to potential bias in ways that undermine their careers.

RACIAL STRESS

The ever-present possibility of discrimination makes working at these firms stressful for Black professionals. Sensing that at least some of their colleagues may harbor racial biases but not being sure which ones, Black professionals can never be sure when they are at risk of being mistreated. This uncertainty can be draining, requiring Black professionals to expend considerable mental energy monitoring and evaluating situations for subtle hints of potential racial unfairness. This vigilance can be onerous. Lionel raised this point during our interview, explaining, "I'd almost trade my experience at [my former law firm] for a blatantly racist place, because it's easier to dodge a bull when you have a cape in your hand than when the lights are off." His imagery of attempting to evade a dangerous bovine in the dark colorfully captures the difficulty of attempting to predict discrimination and the potential peril of failing to avoid it.

As a result, many Black professionals feel that they must stay alert to potential discrimination while proving themselves time and time again by performing flawlessly in every aspect of their work. These extra demands can render these already challenging work environments unbearably stressful.[23] This racial stress consumes precious mental bandwidth and can drain them cognitively, emotionally, and physically, thereby impairing their work performance.[24] It also produces frustration and burnout, contributing to racially disparate rates of self-elimination, as Black professionals choose to quit these firms in search of fairer work environments. Racial stress can even threaten Black professionals' physical and emotional well-being; concerns about discrimination are associated with hypertension and other health problems.[25]

Interviewees described feeling intense stress because they feared that their White colleagues might treat them unfairly. Nakia, an investment banker who worked at a small, minority-owned bank, explained that her job was "so much less stressful" than her prior position at a major Wall Street bank where she had constantly worried about bosses overreacting to her mistakes. Other interviewees spoke of feeling dread in anticipation of informal outings with colleagues away from their offices. Pernell described experiencing anxiety at social gatherings with colleagues from his investment bank, at which he often was the only Black person present. Concerned that his White colleagues might make racially offensive comments when they became intoxicated and perceiving that he had little in common with them, Pernell despaired at the prospect of spending time with them socially.

> I've gotten there many times where you walk into a party and nobody looks like you, and your mind is already set on what time am I getting out of here, what excuse am I going to give if anyone asks where I'm going, how am I going to get through this night, what can I make up to talk about. So from the first twenty seconds of some of the events I went to, I was already in defense mode. And that's just debilitating and painful and it just takes you away from the situation. . . . I would say that's probably the toughest side of Wall Street.

While many of his White counterparts seemed to relish partying with colleagues and clients, attending these outings required Pernell to navigate unfamiliar and deeply uncomfortable social situations. Even if none of Pernell's fears ever came to pass, the stress he experienced in these environments disadvantaged him by impeding his access to useful social capital.

For these reasons, socializing with coworkers does not necessarily provide the same benefits for Black professionals as it does for other workers. While participating in office-related social gatherings generally enables workers to form stronger bonds with one another, many Black professionals who attend such outings leave feeling no closer to their White colleagues.[26] On the contrary, the stressfulness and awkwardness of these encounters can ultimately lead Black professionals to avoid them altogether, further reducing their chances of achieving full inclusion at their firms.[27]

Because the dynamics of stigma anxiety have not been well understood, many Black professionals who experience these challenges internalize them as evidence of their own shortcomings. Some interviewees even criticized themselves for lacking the confidence and social grace to "play the game" and network with colleagues. This sense of self-blame renders social outings with colleagues even more frustrating. For instance, although Pernell knew other Black professionals who experienced similar apprehensions, he blamed his difficulties entirely on himself. He explained, "It was totally on me and I knew it, and it was my own personal insecurities." His critical self-assessment underscores another important drawback of stigma anxiety: people sometimes interpret it as a deficiency of individual Black professionals without considering the legitimacy of their underlying concerns. That Pernell eventually grew more comfortable in racially isolating social outings with work colleagues does not mean that his initial anxiety was unreasonable. Having already had awkward interactions with colleagues in the office, Pernell had every reason to expect more of the same—or worse—in these more informal settings.

RACIAL RETICENCE

One defensive mechanism that Black professionals employ in response to stigma anxiety is what I refer to as racial reticence, which occurs when Black professionals silence themselves to attempt to limit their exposure to discrimination. Black professionals engage in racial reticence in situations where they fear that speaking up or speaking out might be counterproductive due to adverse racial stereotypes of Black people as incompetent, angry, or threatening. But while remaining quiet in potentially risky situations may allow Black professionals to avoid some dangers, it can do them more harm than good by hindering them from obtaining critical opportunities and resources.

Fear of Being Judged Incompetent
Some Black professionals act reticently out of fear of misspeaking in front of potentially racially biased colleagues who may interpret their gaffes as proof that they are unintelligent and incompetent. This concern informs how Black professionals approach various aspects of their jobs, including team meetings, in which the professionals working on particular matters convene to update each other about relevant developments, discuss issues of concern, and plan future actions. These meetings present important opportunities for junior professionals to demonstrate certain valued skills and traits to their senior colleagues, including their analytical abilities, communication skills, and enthusiasm about their work. The impressions that junior professionals make during even relatively brief meetings can have outsized impacts that rival the impact of their performance on substantive work assignments.

Participating at these meetings requires professionals to speak up in front of predominantly White audiences of colleagues and, occasionally, clients. Worried that their colleagues will subject their words to unfair criticism, many Black professionals choose to remain silent during these meetings. Black professionals are not the only people who feel nervous speaking up before senior colleagues and clients; junior professionals of all races grapple with such anxiety. But Black professionals' apprehensions are distinct, and potentially more severe, in that they reflect a fear of being singled out for unfair treatment. Kim, an attorney, described how such concerns led her to take a cautious approach during her team meetings, with unfavorable results. She explained that she only volunteered her thoughts during team meetings when she felt absolutely certain they would be well received, which contributed to a misperception that she was not as dedicated to her work as some of her White peers: "It's not that we're not *engaged*, it's just I feel like some of our [White] counterparts who are much more comfortable say all kinds of ridiculous things, but they sort of get rewarded for saying something. Whereas I feel as if I should be much more thoughtful. So if it comes out, I have thought about it, made sure it's right three times before I make any comment at all, which is sort of—I'm being penalized for my thoughtfulness."

Kim's concerns about her comments being unfairly judged are common; they are consistent with views expressed by Black professionals in previous studies.[28] But as her comment reveals, the adaptive response of reticence during team meetings has a number of downsides. It can result in considerable opportunity costs in missed chances to impress one's colleagues. It can also lead senior colleagues to question a junior professionals' ability and commitment, as senior colleagues can interpret silence as lack of interest or insight. As a result, though it is understandable, racial reticence can lead to the very outcomes that the Black professionals who engage in it hope to avoid. Although Kim's approach might seem prudent given the prevalence of racial bias, in this context it worked to her disadvantage. In her annual review, her senior colleagues criticized her for not speaking enough: "I feel as if I get some of the typical comments that African American attorneys get often. . . . They say 'too quiet,' 'I want you to speak up more,' 'I want you to be a little more aggressive,' 'ask more questions'—those were some of the comments that I got. . . . 'I wasn't contributing'—those sorts of things."

Rachel, a law firm associate who eventually made partner, also discussed the drawbacks of racial reticence. Although Rachel herself did not engage in racial reticence, she observed how it impacted the careers of some of her Black friends and colleagues. She noted that by silencing themselves, these Black attorneys missed out on critical opportunities to impress their partners. "When you don't say anything, then it becomes an issue," Rachel explained. "Then it's like, 'Oh that Black girl over there—I hear she's smart but she just doesn't talk.' And so I think that's how race becomes an issue." Thus, even highly talented Black professionals who perform well can still suffer deficits in trust and rapport with key colleagues if they do not feel comfortable speaking up during meetings and other interactions.

Racial reticence can unwittingly reinforce racial stereotypes, as any colleagues who question Black professionals' intelligence and competence may interpret their silence as proof that they are incapable of contributing to substantive discussions. It also can diminish Black professionals' work performance, as their concerns about being stereotyped as incompetent can lead them to refrain from seeking necessary assistance on difficult assignments. Chinelo, a former law firm associate, explained, "Rather than asking questions or being able to say, 'I don't know,' we hide and struggle on our own. We work doubly hard on challenging assignments trying to figure out on our own because we aren't comfortable saying 'I don't understand,' because we think the consequences might be different for Black people."

Whether or not their underlying concerns are sound, Black professionals' decisions not to seek help can expose them to even greater risks. Workers who are not comfortable accepting help from colleagues may perform worse than others,[29] and this discomfort can be especially detrimental at professional services firms, where performance expectations are not always clear. Chinelo found that her go-it-alone approach undermined her performance and proved to be stressful and time consuming.[30] She explained, "I was struggling with the work . . . It did take me time to get through things. And I did feel very reluctant to ask quote-unquote dumb questions. So I would struggle to find the answers on my own. So . . . my effectiveness and my efficiency really weren't that good." Thus, attempts to avoid racial stereotypes may end up reinforcing them, as they can lead to Black professionals performing worse and taking longer to complete their assignments. In this and other ways, racial reticence can be just as harmful as the anticipated discrimination that triggers it.

Fear of Being the "Angry Black Person"

Concerns that their colleagues presume them to be incompetent are not the only source of stigma anxiety that causes Black professionals to self-silence when they might be better off speaking up or reaching out for help. Apprehension about another racial stereotype—that of Black people as excessively angry and emotional—can also lead to self-silencing.[31] To avoid this stereotype, some Black workers abide by "racialized feelings rules," according to which they feel compelled to conceal their emotions to avoid making colleagues uncomfortable.[32] In a similar vein, some Black professionals are reluctant to assert themselves when they have been treated unfairly. Black female professionals may be especially likely to experience this concern, as they also face gendered stereotypes and expectations that lead people to penalize women for acting assertively.[33] Interviewees described how such concerns made them reluctant to stand up for themselves even when doing so might have been beneficial. Samantha, a former law firm associate, recalled receiving a disproportionate amount of low-quality work assignments early in her career. She explained that rather than object to her treatment, she "didn't bring it up" out of concern that doing so might rub her senior colleagues the wrong way. She contrasted her passivity with the assertive approach that a non-Black colleague of hers used in handling similar situations: "He would turn down assignments and say 'you need to have a paralegal do it, I'm too qualified for that.'" In discussing her own reluctance to use such tactics, Samantha attributed it to her being "on guard because of the 'angry Black female' thing."

Samantha's account illustrates some of the indirect effects of stigma. Deciding how to address unfair work allocations can be difficult for all junior professionals, but it is especially fraught for those who worry that colleagues might view their actions through the warped lenses of racial stereotypes. Samantha's perception that she had less leeway than her colleague to push back against undesirable assignments led her to take an approach that possibly rendered her more susceptible to being saddled with additional low-quality work in the future.

Fear of Seeming Threatening

Some Black male professionals also choose to act less assertively than their White colleagues to avoid triggering stereotypes of Black men as hostile and violent.[34] Timothy, who previously worked at a large law firm, reported that such concerns led him to modify his speech and behavior in interactions with certain colleagues. He explained, "As African Americans, especially males . . . you don't want to come across too strong." Timothy found that this strategy backfired, as his efforts to project a nonthreatening persona resulted in a partner criticizing him for being too "tentative" and "nice" to fit in with the culture of their department, a litigation department whose attorneys were known for being intense and aggressive. Timothy accepted these criticisms and blamed himself for doing "too many mental gymnastics." Although the racial danger that he sought to avoid was a real one and his approach to handling it reasonable, his attempts to avoid Black stereotypes harmed him anyway, by preventing him from projecting the type of professional image valued in his department.

SELF-CONCEALMENT

In addition to their concerns about speaking up about work matters, many Black professionals also feel anxious about the possible consequences of sharing certain personal information with their White colleagues. This concern leads them to engage in self-concealment, a form of impression management in which they intentionally limit their disclosure of details about their personal lives or their authentic personalities in their interactions with non-Black colleagues. Some specifically worry that their colleagues might look down upon some of their distinctively Black social and cultural traits, including that they listen to certain rap music, live in predominantly Black neighborhoods, socialize at Black nightclubs, or belong to Black social organizations.[35] Therefore, they attempt to hide this information through a strategy that is a form of what Erving Goffman termed *covering*, which occurs when members of stigmatized groups attempt to negate adverse biases by concealing or deemphasizing their stigmatized traits.[36]

Some Black professionals engage in a different type of self-concealment as a response to other concerns. Worried that their colleagues might not fully respect them as dignified professionals, they sense that they may face adverse judgments for acting too casually in the office, for example by joining their White counterparts in coarse banter or raucous partying or discussions of their personal lives. These concerns lead them to adopt highly formal interactional styles in which they strive to present themselves as respectable and to conceal information that they believe might cause their White colleagues to judge them adversely. For example, some interviewees explained that they refrain from using profanity or discussing their social lives or romantic relationships, even when their White colleagues routinely do so.

Self-concealment insulates Black professionals from some possible harms, but it is not without its costs and risks.[37] It can further isolate Black professionals, reinforcing their status as outsiders at their firms. In informal work settings where self-disclosure and casual banter are the norm, formal and restrained interactional approaches can set Black professionals apart from their colleagues. Several interviewees described engaging in self-concealment during their interactions with White colleagues, which they acknowledged further limited their access to workplace social capital. Maria, an attorney, came across as outgoing and personable during our interview. But she reported that although she had an active social life and an extensive network of friends, this network did not include any of the White colleagues whom she encountered every day at her firm. Maria explained that she intentionally presented a formal and nonsociable demeanor during her interactions with them: "I don't talk about anything personal with them." Maria also chose not to socialize with them away from the office: "I'm not calling them for drinks on a Saturday like 'oh, let's hang out.' My Black friend I would, but not the other ones." Maria recognized that her approach ran afoul of office norms and counter to insights she recently had come upon while reading a book written by a successful Black Wall Street investment banker: "Ironically, I'm reading this book by Carla Harris called 'Expect to Win,' and . . . she was saying that Black women usually—we put up a wall. We only want to show you this much of us, so we are not going to engage in that type of conversations that would then allow us to have those personal relationships you just asked about. So part of that would be my fault."

Although self-concealment is an understandable reaction to

the discomforting conditions of racial isolation, as Maria noted, Black professionals who practice it can miss out on opportunities to develop valuable social capital. Sharing personal information is a key component of building and maintaining relationships, so people who are not comfortable doing so are at a social disadvantage.[38] To the extent that relationships are "a process of gradually escalating self-disclosure," as one scholar of race in the workplace posited, self-concealment can be antithetical to forming bonds with colleagues.[39] By conforming to abstract norms of professionalism instead of the actual cultures of their work groups, Black professionals who self-conceal may stick out instead of fitting in. Thus, in attempting to avoid being stigmatized, they suffer other potential harms and opportunity costs. In this manner, the stigma anxiety brought on by conditions at elite firms leads some Black professionals to act in ways that reinforce racial disparities. As her White colleagues bonded and developed goodwill with one another, Maria likely stood out as less familiar and perhaps even aloof and less collegial. There is no way to know for sure whether Maria would have had a better experience had she been more comfortable self-disclosing (she reported being miserable during her time at the firm and left after two years of working there), but more camaraderie and social support certainly could have made her time there more tolerable.

The decision to engage in self-concealment in some instances stems from Black professionals' negative experiences with White peers prior to joining their firms. Maria explained that over the course of her life she had had very few White friends and more than her share of unfriendly interactions with White peers. She had overheard offensive comments made by White high school classmates—especially after she was admitted to an Ivy League college—and she recalled White college classmates making racially offensive comments in and out of class. Aside from classroom interactions, Maria had very little contact with her White classmates in college. In fact, she graduated from her predominantly White college without making a single White friend. "I don't really have any White friends from [Ivy League College]," she explained. "As strange as most people think that is, I really just *don't*, because I didn't integrate with them." This personal background may help explain why Maria was not more comfortable or interested in interacting with White colleagues at the firm. Her experiences are consistent with broader research demonstrating that the interracial relationships and interactions that people have earlier in life shape their racial attitudes and the racial demographics of their social networks as adults.[40]

Criticisms from Other Black Professionals

Stigma anxiety subjects Black professionals to criticisms and other risks when it leads them to act in ways that deviate from workplace norms and expectations. Indeed, even Black professionals at times judge their friends' and colleagues' adaptive responses to stigma anxiety harshly. This occurs because individual members of stigmatized groups have different levels of stigma consciousness and widely diverging views about the likelihood that they will encounter racial mistreatment.[41] Some are more likely to notice potential evidence of discrimination and to interpret acts as discriminatory even with little evidence, while others regularly overlook possible evidence of bias and do not attribute incidents to discrimination even with fairly compelling evidence.[42] Because evidence of discrimination is often ambiguous, any two Black professionals might interpret the same situation differently and reach vastly different conclusions about the role of race.[43] Those who downplay the likely impact of race in some instances find fault with those who are more stigma conscious.

Rachel, the attorney, demonstrated this tendency in describing the struggles with racial anxiety of her Black mentees at the firm. "I think a lot of them just got so caught up in their personal stuff that they really just couldn't be regular people around partners," she explained. "And that lack of self-confidence, that anxiety—I think it makes partners uncomfortable." For this reason, Rachel considered racial reticence a losing strategy, even if she sympathized with her colleagues' concerns. "I'm certainly not saying that this is a utopian society," she added. "But I also think that we've got a responsibility to just let it go and be ourselves." Brett, a midlevel law firm associate, spoke about friends of his who engaged in self-concealment due to stigma anxiety. "I felt like I fit in a whole lot better," he said, "than my friends who felt like we can't drink around the [White] lawyers because Black people are held to a higher standard or something." Brett criticized these attorneys for approaching White colleagues "as if it's us against them" and mocked them for what he interpreted as unjustified paranoia. This anxiety-induced self-concealment likely undermined Brett's friends' careers by further increasing their discomfort and isolation at their firms. Prisca, an attorney, similarly took issue with other Black professionals who were concerned about whether their colleagues covertly held racial biases, complaining that "Black people spend too much time trying to get in White people's heads."

Even though their accounts are secondhand interpretations and in some instances rather uncharitable to their Black colleagues, less stigma-anxious Black professionals like Brett and Rachel may be best positioned to assess the impact of stigma anxiety on other Black professionals. They gain insights into their Black colleagues' and friends' anxieties about racial stigma through conversations with them and then observe the effects of their stigma anxiety as they witness them engaging in racial risk management strategies. Aware of the vast differences between their perspectives on the racial climates of their firms and those of their more stigma-conscious colleagues, they were uniquely situated to describe how attempting to navigate concerns about racism can hinder Black professionals' careers.

Other interviewees also saw Black colleagues engage in self-concealment that appeared to be counterproductive. Regina, a consultant at a Big 3 management consulting firm, noted that some colleagues "struggle[d] with their racial identity" at the firm and "distinguish[ed] between who they are professionally and who they are personally, [with] very significant differences in those two personalities." This approach worked to their disadvantage by making them seem awkward and inauthentic. Regina explained, "I think if you don't bring your authentic self [to workplace interactions], over time you're going to be inconsistent, you're not going to be happy, people are going to see that, they're not going to be happy with you." Regina's perception that Black colleagues who engaged in self-concealment suffered worse outcomes at her firm aligns with research establishing that authenticity in conversations can help people form friendships and other enduring ties.[44]

Beth, a law firm partner, was especially critical of Black female attorneys who were reluctant to speak up in meetings and during interactions with White colleagues. Speaking from her perspective as a partner, she emphasized the importance of associates being comfortable and confident in their interactions with partners: "As a partner, you really need to trust that the people who work for you are competent and that they are going to handle their business and take what you give them and run with it. Because as a partner, you are going to have to sign off on some things that you haven't had time to look over. So . . . you don't want someone who's afraid of their own shadow. You don't want a 'Nervous Nelly.'" She asserted that for this reason, partners are less likely to entrust quality assignments to associates who self-silence: "If you're not engaged—or there's the appearance that you're not engaged— you're not going to get the projects that require the heavy lifting.

Because they need self-starters. Because that partner is going to feel like someone would have to be available to hover over you to tell you what to do every twenty seconds."

Beth connected self-silencing to long-standing folk wisdom embraced by many Black Americans (she explained that "the old saying in our community is 'Don't let the proof that you're an idiot come out of your own mouth'"), which she felt was maladaptive at elite firms. She described this self-silencing as a form of self-sabotage: "Black women who are too worried about themselves . . . hurt themselves before others even get a chance to. Because the worse thing that's going to happen is that you're going to be where you started off (if the partner isn't impressed with you). But instead, you've effectively shut your own self out and that's the stupidest thing that I've ever heard of."

Beth claimed that many Black women had the talent and opportunities to thrive at elite firms but undermined their careers by behaving uncharacteristically passively on the job. "A lot of what holds us back is us," she insisted. "Because the bravado that I love about Black women—that we have—we don't bring to [our firm]. What stops us from getting where we want to go sometimes is really us, it's our problem." She contrasted this with her observations of White male associates who, free from the burdens of stigma anxiety, were able to take better advantage of workplace interactions: "I can't tell you how many young White men say stupid things to me all day. And I just say 'Unh-unh. That doesn't even make sense. Next.' You can tell that it affects them, but it doesn't stop them from coming back and contributing the next day."

Beth may be right to denounce racial reticence as a suboptimal career strategy and to point out that it does Black professionals a disservice, but her attribution of blame and responsibility overlooks the complex causes that lead Black professionals to engage in this adaptive response to racial stigma. Black professionals adopt these defensive and coping mechanisms in racially threatening contexts where they are understandably anxious about potential unfair treatment. Blaming them for their stigma anxiety while ignoring the circumstances that cause it absolves firms of their responsibility to improve workplace conditions. That even someone as familiar with these challenges and strongly committed to issues of racial equity as Beth would take such a narrow and unsympathetic view of racial reticence suggests that misperceptions about stigma anxiety are widespread and reveals the urgent need for greater awareness.

Conclusion

For Black professionals, the *risk* of discrimination at elite firms can impede and even derail their careers regardless of whether they personally experience discrimination. Long-standing racial disparities and perceived discrepancies in the treatment of other employees can lead Black professionals to engage in racial risk management strategies that, while sparing them from some forms of mistreatment, further limit their access to career capital. Racial stress, racial reticence, and self-concealment are reasonable responses to potentially risky situations, but they come with unintended costs and consequences. These adaptive responses to stigma anxiety can be misinterpreted as evidence of professional shortcomings or personal problems. When Black professionals decide not to speak up at team meetings, colleagues may misread this as conveying lack of interest or insight. When Black professionals choose not to share personal information, their colleagues may question their interpersonal skills and perhaps their ability to handle client-facing responsibilities. As I explain in this book's conclusion, there are no easy solutions for addressing these dynamics, but recognizing and understanding them may be an important first step to limiting their impact.

3

White Culture and Black Professionals

While stigma anxiety arises from Black professionals' concerns about racial bias, the other form of racial discomfort, social alienation, is not directly connected to racial bias at all. It stems instead from a different, less obvious source: cultural capital, the cultural tastes, knowledge, and experiences that people accumulate over the course of their lives.[1] Cultural capital structures people's daily lives in varied and far-reaching ways.[2] It encompasses, among other things, the sports that people play and follow, the places where they vacation, the brands of the clothing they wear, the bars and restaurants they frequent, the music they listen to, and the television shows and podcasts they discuss with friends. These traits can influence whether any two people form friendships with each other or become members of the same social groups.[3] People tend to gravitate toward and associate with others who share similar tastes and interests.[4] Such shared cultural traits often make interactions more enjoyable; with them, it is easier for people to engage each other in small talk, and this small talk more often leads to rapport and friendship.[5] On the flip side, people who have dissimilar traits are far less likely to form close social bonds. Because they have less in common with each other, it can be more difficult for them to develop rapport.

This dynamic advantages members of the majority group present in any given setting, as they are more likely to share cultural capital in common with other people, while marginalizing people from underrepresented groups, who are more likely to have dissimilar cultural capital. As I explain, at elite firms differences in Black and White professionals' cultural capital shape workplace interactions in ways that advantage many White professionals while excluding and further marginalizing many Black professionals.[6]

Cultural Traits as Professional Resources

In employment settings, cultural traits serve as bridges of inclusion for some employees while creating boundaries that exclude others. Shared cultural traits can provide access to valuable workplace social capital in the form of office friendships and relationships with sponsors and mentors. This shared cultural common ground helps colleagues develop rapport with each other by enabling them to more easily and enjoyably converse with each other at work and socialize together away from the office.[7] The resulting social bonds provide some professionals with valuable professional advantages over others.[8]

At elite professional services firms, shared cultural traits provide advantages to some professionals even before they are hired. Each year during hiring season, firms invite the most promising entry-level job seekers to visit their offices for interviews with lineups of professionals. In some industries these interviews often involve extensive small talk about interviewees' personal and educational backgrounds and the items listed in the "interests" section of their résumés.[9] In assessing and ranking these potential future colleagues, interviewers regularly privilege those whose cultural traits match their own, a process that business professor Lauren Rivera has termed "cultural matching."[10]

After they have been hired, professionals who share cultural capital with colleagues enjoy greater access to valuable workplace social capital. Michael, a former investment banker who now runs a successful start-up company, explained that "having common interests" and sharing "some kind of common thread" with senior colleagues were critical for developing relationships with mentors and sponsors. Brandon, an attorney, agreed, positing that for building relationships with partners, "there's just no substitute for commonalities." Leonard, an attorney, sensed that cultural common ground was especially important at elite law firms, which as a rule employed an overabundance of highly talented junior attorneys: "All the [associates] have the ability. . . . So what's the basis for advancement? Like anything else, it's always going to come down, to a certain extent, to relationships, interpersonal identification, even formal organizations: be it a wine club [or] be it people who—I hate to use the example, but it's so true—people who play golf or tennis together." As Leonard recognized, cultural common ground can sustain interpersonal bonds that boost professionals' careers. Coworkers who have rapport with one another are more likely to help each other professionally.[11] In these highly competitive firms, where differences in performance are often marginal and subject to interpretation, this preferential treatment can advantage them decisively.

All professionals have strong personal incentives to privilege culturally similar colleagues (and potential colleagues). Work in these firms can be difficult and unpleasant. Challenging workloads, assignments that are either stressful or tedious, and highly demanding clients and bosses are all too common. As working alongside culturally similar colleagues can make these conditions more tolerable, many professionals try to do so when they have the opportunity. Lerone, who worked at a Wall Street investment bank, explained that for this reason he himself privileged applicants with whom he shared certain background experiences and cultural frames of reference.

It's something I actually look for when I interview, to a certain extent, for interns. It's, "Who do I feel comfortable working with late at night?" You're going to sit next to somebody for 10 to 15 hours of your day for every day of the week for a couple years . . . and you want to make sure the person you're sitting next to is . . . someone you can connect with and feel comfortable next to. And I think that translates into, "What are your shared experiences? . . . Who do I feel comfortable working next to because of that shared experience? So that when I make a joke, they get that joke. So that when I'm working late at night and go to drinks with them, they understand where I'm coming from."

Rebecca, a consultant at a large firm, explained the value of working with culturally similar colleagues in comparable terms, referring to the well-known "airport" or "airplane" standard of rapport and compatibility. She stated that because professionals "spend so much time with [their colleagues] in the course of a week," she evaluated job candidates in part by asking herself, "If I'm stuck in an airport for eight hours, are you someone I want to hang out with?"

In acknowledging that they privilege culturally similar applicants for purely self-serving reasons, Lerone's and Rebecca's explanations for homophilic favoritism differ from the classic academic account of this behavior. In her influential theory of homosocial reproduction, organizational scholar Rosabeth Moss Kanter posited that supervisors privilege workers who are similar to themselves because they more often presume that those workers possess certain intangible characteristics relevant to their jobs, such as dependability and good judgment.[12] Under this theory, decision makers who favor similar colleagues are driven to do so by meritocratic motives to hire the workers they believe will perform best for their companies, though their judgments are distorted by their subjective self-referential biases. By contrast, Lerone and Rebecca make clear that professionals also prefer culturally similar others simply because they find them more enjoyable to be around. Taking into account how self-serving motives shape personnel decisions thus provides for a clearer understanding of the long-observed tendency of workplace homophily.

The Cultural Milieus of Elite Firms

Cultural traits do not have intrinsic value. Their usefulness is context specific and determined mainly by the traits and values of the people present in any particular setting.[13] In most instances, the cultural traits of members of dominant groups have the most value and influence. In workplaces these traits become informally institutionalized, influencing everything from the content of small talk in everyday office encounters to the choice of venues for happy hours and other social outings. This is a highly decentralized process. Even within work organizations, different cultural traits have more or less value in different settings depending on the preferences of the people present in a particular relevant office, department, work team, or informal clique.

To gain full inclusion in workplace networks, workers at times must demonstrate some amount of comfort and familiarity with the cultural capital dominant in these settings during small talk and other informal interactions. This is true at elite firms, where possessing the right type of this cultural knowledge can make it much easier for junior professionals to fit in with and impress their colleagues. Wayne, an attorney, discussed some of the many ways that associates at his firm needed to draw from their cultural tool kits to bond with colleagues and gain social acceptance.

For example, attending happy hours, how you conduct yourself at those happy hours—what are the topics of conversation? What are the things you should be up to speed on in the news? What type of places do you like to go to outside of the firm? Also, what types of bars, what type of restaurants—how do you conduct yourself at those restaurants? Are you cultured enough to understand the different things that are on the menu at an exotic restaurant? Can you pronounce the sushi? People hold you to a certain cultural standard that assumes a certain level of sophistication.

These topics might seem whimsical and unimportant, but professionals who lack the requisite cultural traits can find it harder to develop social capital. Wayne recalled seeing some associates who lacked the right cultural capital become essentially discredited for making comments or voicing opinions that were deemed illegitimate. He observed, "[Other attorneys are] judgmental if your preferences are different. . . . If people sort of said anything that was in the realm of the unexpected, it's almost like they were written out of the conversation."

Even matters as seemingly frivolous as sports interests, pop culture references, and nightlife preferences can carry professional consequences. In work settings where many professionals enjoy golf, golf can influence everyday discourse and access to relationships.[14] In such settings, being able to discuss golf knowledgeably helps workers develop rapport with colleagues. Those who can join their colleagues on golf outings enjoy valuable opportunities to network and bond with them. People in these work groups who do not know much about golf may feel compelled to take up the sport to better fit in with colleagues and avoid being marginalized.

These culture-related office social dynamics can contribute to inequitable employment impacts and outcomes, as shown in the diagram below. When some workers secure disproportionate resources on the basis of their shared cultural repertoires and social backgrounds, other workers suffer competitive disadvantages.[15] These processes have winners and losers, and because of race-

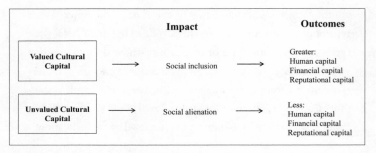

Effects of cultural capital on professional career

related cultural differences and the skewed racial demographics of these firms, Black professionals often are among those who lose.

Race and Culture

Cultural traits are in some respects personal and idiosyncratic, but they are also informed by social identity characteristics such as gender, age, social class, and race.[16] When patterns emerge such that dominant and marginalized groups have different cultural traits, these differences can reinforce existing inequalities. For example, class- and gender-based cultural differences both contribute to workplace inequality: when workers from affluent backgrounds bond over their past participation in expensive leisure activities or when male workers alienate women by centering workplace discussions around "sports talk," workers from less privileged backgrounds and women become further isolated and marginalized.[17]

While these class and gender dynamics have produced considerable research, the similar effects of race-related cultural differences have received far less attention. This neglect is understandable. The juncture of race, culture, and inequality is especially fraught, tainted by its association with pathology-based arguments that essentialize and denigrate certain racial groups and their members.[18] But although no racial group's cultural traits are intrinsically superior, in White-dominated employment contexts the cultural traits possessed by White professionals become especially valuable. And even though neither Black professionals nor White professionals are culturally monolithic, distinct racial patterns in tastes, interests, and sensibilities are evident across a broad array of life activities.[19]

Consider television, for example. In recent years, shows such as *Empire* and *Love & Hip-Hop Atlanta* have been highly popular among Black viewers while receiving only lukewarm interest from White audiences.[20] In 2017 none of the five shows most popular among Black viewers—all of which featured predominantly Black casts—were among the programs most widely watched by White Americans.[21] This divide is evident even with respect to the various series of Bravo's *Real Housewives* franchise. While Black audiences mainly tune in to watch the all-Black casts of *Real Housewives of Atlanta* and *Real Housewives of Potomac*, White viewers instead primarily watch the nearly all-White *Real Housewives of Beverly Hills* and *Real Housewives of New York*.[22] This cultural distance is not a recent phenomenon; a similar divide existed in the 1990s, during the formative years of some of today's professionals. At that time *Seinfeld*, the single most highly watched show among White viewers, ranked no higher than fiftieth among Black viewers and in some seasons did not even crack Black audiences' top 100 shows.[23] *Friends* and other shows wildly popular among White audiences also drew low Black viewership. Conversely, the shows that were most popular among Black viewers, such as *Living Single*, *New York Undercover*, and *Moesha*, were not even among the eighty shows most watched by all viewers.[24]

Similar, though less quantifiable, patterns are also evident in many other cultural domains, including sports, music, nightlife activities, and comedy.[25] These differences can also manifest through social media. One especially prominent testament to the persistent cultural and social distinctions between Black and White Americans is "Black Twitter," an influential subculture of (mostly) Black Twitter users who use the medium to engage each other about issues of interest to Black Americans.[26] The content and style of the banter and viral memes on Black Twitter reflect cultural knowledge familiar to many Black professionals and foreign to many White audiences. Similar patterns are evident on Instagram.

The Cultural Common Ground Problem

Thus, Black and White professionals often begin their careers with different cultural capital.[27] This dissimilitude disadvantages Black professionals because their prospects at these firms depend on their relationships with their White colleagues. To access opportunities and relationships, Black professionals at times must adapt to White cultural traits; those who are unable or unwilling to do so may suffer. James, an associate working at his third law firm, described experiencing these difficulties. Like many Black professionals, James often found informal interactions with White colleagues somewhat uncomfortable because of their divergent backgrounds and interests.

> If there's a big meeting, you might see a bunch of African Americans in one part of the room talking to each other. That's noticeable—it's probably because of the comfort level. It's different with the White partners. I don't have the same experiences as them. I didn't play golf growing up. I didn't have much to offer to a conversation that was talking about how [golfer Arnold] Palmer was doing. . . . It also goes to where people vacation, stuff like that. The chit-chat varies according to whose experiences are being

discussed. . . . If African Americans don't have those experiences, then often times we won't get as close to the partners.

James's observation captures the subtle manner in which seemingly innocuous culturally infused interactions can contribute to inequality. His difficulties are consistent with broader racial patterns: Black people constitute only an estimated 3 percent of all golfers and 7 percent of all Professional Golfers' Association viewers.[28] James described how the ensuing social distance at his firm limited Black associates' access to premium work opportunities, producing disparities in assignments. He explained, "It's not racial, but the appearance is that the White attorneys will get a lot of the more posh assignments that can lead to greater things." This is an example of the cultural common ground problem in action.

Bert, an attorney, experienced similar difficulties at his law firm. He recalled watching helplessly as a White classmate developed an easy rapport with a top partner in their department, while his efforts to do the same were less fruitful: "There's one senior partner in the group who's probably in his early 50s. I worked with him repeatedly. I try to make small talk with him, and it's fine, but not much comes from it. Whereas my peer, who's a White male associate who grew up in suburban New York in a town like the partner lives in—his father was a partner in a law firm, he went to good schools. . . . They talk for hours about things." Such long, intimate conversations help professionals build social capital, and they influence workers' sense of belonging. Bert worried that the rapport between his two White colleagues eventually would give his peer a competitive advantage. He explained, "I think that makes a difference because the partner feels more comfortable about this guy, because they've chit-chatted about whatever it is they've chit-chatted about, and he's like, 'Oh, he's a good guy.' . . . Seems cliché but it does happen."

Sharing a common racial identity is not enough to ensure that any two people will enjoy such rapport. But being a White male increases the likelihood of finding senior colleagues with similar cultural traits. As Michael, the former investment banker, observed, "It's easier if you're at a place where you're in the majority—you're going to have more people like you who share the same experiences, who come from the same background. And so the numbers are in your favor." In the competitive quest for scarce career capital, this advantage can be decisive.

Cultural and social differences also limit Black professionals' access to relationships with their White peers. Brianne, an attorney, reported that her White colleagues frequently peppered their workplace banter with pop culture references that she found unfamiliar. Two particular shows, *Friends* and *Seinfeld*, seemed to be constant frames of reference for her White coworkers as sources of nostalgia and humor. Brianne explained that she had not watched either show growing up because they had aired at the same time as *Martin* and *Living Single*, shows with predominantly Black casts that were more popular among Black viewers. These and similar differences made Brianne feel like an outsider at her firm and made her less interested in engaging in small talk with colleagues. Other interviewees reported similar experiences. Alan, an attorney, quit his first law firm in frustration within two years of starting, having not formed a single close relationship with any of his colleagues. He attributed this social isolation to certain cultural differences between him and his colleagues. "Part of that could be cultural, as I look back on it," he noted. "I'm not familiar with certain movies that the associates would talk about or certain experiences." Lionel, a former law firm associate who now works in-house at a major corporation, recalled feeling alienated from the White attorneys in his group throughout his six-year tenure at a large law firm. He explained that his lack of commonalities with his colleagues repeatedly caused him great stress and left him feeling like a perennial outsider. He described how this social dynamic unfolded during the initial meetings that partners convened whenever they assembled a team of attorneys to work on a new deal for a client.

> You have these start-of-the-deal meetings . . . and the connections have started to form between the senior associates and the juniors. They've already formed between the senior [associate] and the partner . . . It reinforces this outsider mentality that there's something different or awkward about me because I'm not fitting [in]. "I can't think of the right things to say, I don't have the background, they're all very comfortable and, oh my god, what am I doing?" I don't know about you, but once that starts for me, there's a downhill slope . . . That happened to me for *years* at [the Firm]. Drove me insane.

Lionel's reflection reveals the considerable psychological harms of this cultural alienation. The "outsider mentality" that he described also has negative indirect consequences. The stress and frustration that it entails can lead Black professionals to abandon aspirations for long-term careers at their firms in search of more inclusive work settings where they can feel more comfortable.

These cultural dynamics also disadvantage many Black professionals outside the office, at both organized firm-sponsored activities and more impromptu gatherings. While some professionals find these outings fun opportunities to bond with each other and blow off steam, many Black professionals find them challenging and frustrating. Cultural differences that are not even apparent in the office can become salient there, further alienating Black professionals. Interviewees complained that work outings routinely were organized according to the cultural preferences that their White colleagues took for granted, with little regard for the divergent tastes of other workers. Cathy, a former management consultant who now works at a Wall Street investment bank, recognized the potential value of attending these gatherings but expressed frustration about their racial and gender skews. "People feel at ease when you come into their world [and] you start to relate to them," she noted. "A problem is that it seems like the burden always falls on us as minorities or women." Similarly, Kevon explained that while he and other Black consultants had to put aside their own cultural preferences and try to acclimate themselves to those of their colleagues in order to fit in, many of his White male counterparts were able to adapt to the office's cultural milieu more seamlessly: "You don't have to change who you are if you're the guy who wants to go and get a bunch of beers, or you play golf and you do all these things, and you go [to the firm] and, wow, those are the same things that the senior people like to do. Or the people managing you like to do. . . . These guys—they don't really have to change who they are that much."

As Kevon recognized, in order to take full advantage of these opportunities to build social capital, many Black professionals must in some ways "change who they are" in accordance with the preferences and values of their White colleagues. This imposition can be subtle, but over time it fuels alienation and resentment. Wayne, a former associate at a large Washington, DC, law firm, voiced these frustrations: "There's another layer of complication, stress, almost like another layer of the job that you have to go through if you're not comfortable—for example, if you don't like to go out and drink beer. There's small annoyances. If you go to a firm event you know there's going to be shitty music. That's just the way it is. You ignore it but why should you? Why is it that there are only certain genres? . . . What it meant to go out and have a good time was very monolithic." Although Wayne chose to endure these outings despite his misgivings, some of his Black colleagues decided to forego them altogether. Wayne said, "I'm sure there are certain people who have a very difficult time adapting to that or have no desire to adapt and don't think it's worth the price."

Greta shared that she and many other Black professionals at her Wall Street investment bank avoided office social outings for these very reasons. She stated that White professionals in her department regularly went out for drinks with each other after work and seemed to enjoy these outings, which they used to bond and share information.[29] Greta explained, "That's where a lot of socializing happens, that's where a lot of conversations happen." Many of the group's Black professionals found the gatherings less comfortable and enjoyable and therefore either avoided them or only attended grudgingly. "We [Black professionals] know there's a game and we just don't want to play it," she said. "And the game is harder for us." Because these get-togethers reflected the unfamiliar cultural and social preferences of her White colleagues, Greta found them laborious and challenging. Accustomed to socializing in different, predominantly Black social spaces, Greta preferred styles of music and conversation very different than those of her work group's bar outings. This social alienation disadvantaged Greta professionally by further hindering her from developing relationships and rapport with White mentors and potential allies in her group.

Other Black professionals reported similar difficulties. Nakia, an investment banker who previously worked at a Wall Street bank, remembered being bemused by some of her White former colleagues' social preferences. She was particularly taken aback by their frequent and heavy consumption of alcohol and the extent to which it shaped their workplace banter and camaraderie. "There were so many cultural differences [relating to] what they did on the weekend," she recalled. While these workers enjoyed the benefits of camaraderie, Nakia felt alienated and excluded: "To me it always just made me feel like I didn't belong." Nakia eventually left the bank to work at a far less prestigious but more racially diverse one.

That informal outings and interactions intensify Black professionals' alienation suggests that, perhaps counterintuitively, Black professionals may fare worst in settings with sociable office cultures. The more White professionals spend time networking and socializing with one another through activities and conversations tailored to their own cultural preferences, the greater the relative isolation and alienation of Black professionals and other social outsiders.

Distinct from Racial Bias

The tendency to gravitate toward similar others is a universal behavior; as Lerone and Rebecca explained, Black professionals also engage in it when their circumstances permit. But within these firms it is usually White people who are able to act on the basis of homophily and therefore White people who benefit from it. On the surface, this homophily-driven behavior can resemble racial bias. After all, racial bias can manifest itself in similar ways. Like homophily, racial bias can involve positive orientations toward other people on the basis of shared traits, such as when White people presume other White people to be more competent and trustworthy than people from other racial groups.[30] Racial bias can also disadvantage individuals from underrepresented racial groups who have nonconforming cultural traits, for example when it leads White employers to discriminate against Black workers who wear distinctively Black hairstyles (e.g., dreadlocks and Afros).[31] Like the cultural dynamics that cause social alienation, racial bias can be subtle and need not involve any malicious intent; implicit bias is thought to be subconscious and almost automatic.[32] So when a White professional privileges a White colleague or a group of White professionals socialize in ways that exclude their Black colleagues, it can be difficult to rule out racial bias as a contributing factor.

But although cultural homophily is a form of in-group preference that at times has a racial impact, it operates on the basis of culture, not race. This distinction is subtle but important. Any cultural trait can serve as a basis for inclusion or alienation, including some that are not at all associated with race. The cultural traits that interviewees found problematic at their firms—including heavy beer consumption, golf, and familiarity with certain television comedies—may disproportionately exclude Black professionals, but they are not intrinsically intertwined with racial identity the way that other cultural traits are, such as traditionally Black hairstyles or involvement in Black fraternities and sororities. And there is little reason to believe that White professionals who bond with each other over shared cultural interests do so as a sinister pretextual means of subordinating Black professionals.

Interviewees who reported feeling alienated by being constantly subjected to their White colleagues' cultural preferences did not regard this problem as covert racial discrimination by proxy. On the contrary, they regularly distinguished between social alienation and racial discrimination. Many of the interviewees who struggled most with alienation made clear that they did not consider their firms racist or their colleagues biased. Brandon, an attorney, experienced considerable alienation on the basis of culture at his firm but considered these challenges to be fundamentally different than racial bias. He explained that although "there's definitely lots of times when I felt that I was on the outside looking in," "it's hard for me to levy a racism accusation." Wayne, who described experiencing social alienation at his former law firm, also took pains to emphasize that he did not consider racial bias to be a major source of disadvantage for Black associates: "Do I feel that generally at the firm that people said, 'That person is Black, therefore I'm not going to work with them' or 'They must not be very bright, so I'm not going to give them work'? No." Greta, too, emphasized that although she felt alienated around her White colleagues, she "never felt an experience with someone against me because of my race."

Aja, one of a few Black associates among hundreds of attorneys in her office, spoke of "feeling like an outcast" on "an island of my own." She explained that aside from one other Black associate, "I don't really talk to anybody here." Like Brandon and Greta, Aja declined to attribute her difficulties to racial bias: "I just don't feel plugged in. . . . [T]hat would be the only thing that I could say would be race but then it's not racism, it's just that I'm different, and I have no idea how to fit in here. I have no idea how to be the person that you want to drink with."

These interviewees not only differentiated alienation from racial bias, they regarded it as a bigger impediment to their careers. Lerone, the Wall Street trader, believed that certain White senior colleagues had passed him over for lucrative opportunities that they instead steered to less deserving White colleagues, not because of racial bias but because of homophily. He attributed his treatment to cultural and social—as opposed to purely racial—factors.

> Looking back on it now, I want to say it was culture. . . . It was very much a 'friend recommendation' thing—that's how you got on there. . . . I don't think all of that was race. I think it was much more 'What do you have in common? Are we all from the same country club? Do we all celebrate the same Jewish holidays?' It was much more a function of that than race. . . . It's race but it's also culture. . . . I think that translates into, 'What are your shared experiences?' But I think race plays a factor in the fact that you may have little shared experiences depending on race.

Lerone's account captures the nuanced nature of culture-based exclusion, in which racial differences and cultural differences often overlap. Whether or not his assessment of his colleagues' motives is accurate, the explanation he offers seems plausible, and it is not contingent upon racial bias.

Chinelo, the former attorney, emphasized that she attributed her negative experiences at her former firm to social factors and not racial bias. "I came to think of it as being less about race and more about affinity," she explained. "It's not that people necessarily look at you and say, 'Oh, you're Black so you are inferior.' . . . You do stuff for your friends—that's human nature." In explaining why she did not interpret her difficulties as racial discrimination, Chinelo recalled an incident in which she was a member of an in-group that inadvertently excluded another colleague, a White male associate. After winning a difficult pro bono case, the rest of the team, all of whom were women, chose a celebratory outing in line with their cultural preferences and forgot to invite the male associate: "The women decided to have tea at [an upscale tea room] when we realized we had forgotten the guy. We had left him out. We realized that we had discriminated against him. This is how it happens! . . . A bunch of people who have things in common get together—they gravitate to each other and exclude people." Though not at all equivalent to the broader patterns that consistently marginalize many Black professionals, this tea party demonstrates how even seemingly innocuous workplace behavior centered around common cultural interests and tastes can exclude nongroup members in the absence of bias. Thus, even if it were somehow possible to eradicate racial bias altogether, the problems described in this chapter would likely persist.

BLACK BENEFICIARIES

Further underscoring the distinction between cultural alienation and racial bias is the fact that several Black professionals in my sample either benefited from cultural homophily themselves or knew Black colleagues who did.[33] Lerone spoke of watching a Black summer intern at his investment bank bond with a vice president in his group over their shared passion for golf. Lerone recalled being disappointed, but not especially surprised, when as a result of that relationship the summer intern later received a job offer over a non-Black intern whom Lerone considered to be more deserving. Although the situation that Lerone observed, in which a Black professional received preferential treatment on the basis of his cultural repertoire, may not be common, that it happens at all illustrates the difference between these culture-based processes and racial bias.

Alan, who had suffered social isolation at his previous law firm, benefited from cultural homophily himself when he met senior colleagues who shared his interest in sports. Alan, who had grown up in Jamaica, described how his cultural background paid social dividends when he temporarily moved to the firm's London office: "I feel like I could have lived in London, *easily*. Because I made more friends there in the short time that I was [there] then I did the whole time here. . . . That's why I go back to the whole thing about culture. Because growing up in Jamaica, we had cricket, we had soccer. So I was talking to partners and people about cricket. . . . And it made me realize, 'Wow, if I could only talk about golf and my handicap!'" This cultural common ground turned Alan from an outsider to an insider. There is no way to know whether Alan would have had a better career in the London office, but this insider status could have at least spared him some of the harms of alienation.

Stacey, an attorney, benefited from having certain cultural traits in common with some of her White colleagues. Soon after joining the firm, she befriended several White women in her associate class through their shared love of Broadway musicals. More importantly, she was also able to leverage this cultural capital to bond with a partner in her department. As her relationship with the partner blossomed into a friendship, the partner gave Stacey useful advice and a steady flow of high-quality assignments (Stacey described her as "really instrumental in getting me good work"). Stacey's cultural capital also helped her establish rapport with another, even more powerful partner, during a formal firm event. She explained, "I knew that he liked art [so] I sat down with him at a big dinner, sort of a Black-tie event, and I said, 'I really want to tell you about this exhibit that I saw recently when I was in New York.' All the other partners were looking around and finally someone said, 'I thought you were talking about a *trial* exhibit' and he said, 'No. She knows where my heart is really at; she's talking about an exhibit at the Metropolitan Museum of Art.'" This partner became a friend and a sponsor. He gave Stacey tickets to fine arts shows and entertainment events in their city and also provided her with premium work opportunities. As Stacey acknowledged, she did not gain access to this highly useful relationship through her work performance or any job-relevant characteristics. Instead, she formed it simply by "carrying on an intelligent conversation that had to do with something I was genuinely interested in." In this way, her cultural capital enabled her to benefit from the very social dynamics that subject many other Black professionals to social alienation.

The Double Disadvantage of Race and Gender

Notwithstanding Stacey's positive experiences, the problems of cultural alienation and exclusion tend to be especially salient for Black women, who face these disadvantages on account of both race and gender. At elite firms, as in many other work settings, the cultural traits of White *men* in particular disproportionately dictate the flow of conversations and other workplace interactions.[34] These traits often are distinctively gendered, involving stereotypically masculine tastes that alienate and exclude women. For example, sports and sports talk are well-known mainstays of workplace culture that often facilitate male bonding while marginalizing women.[35] Nakia referred to sports talk as "the default conversation" at her former investment bank, a description that undoubtedly would have rung true to many other interviewees. Similarly, Cathy criticized male colleagues at her investment bank for failing to recognize that "the world doesn't revolve around baseball and football" and for not considering how their incessant sports banter "could discourage some women." Aja complained that sports were such a prominent feature of workplace interactions at her law firm that her lack of interest impeded her from bonding with partners. "I don't talk sports," she explained. "If it's going to be a buddy-buddy thing, it's who they want to drink with, and I can't share a beer with you and talk about the [local NFL team] because I don't watch football." She noted that some partners even took potential clients hunting as part of their business development efforts. The choice of hunting, a pastime almost exclusively popular among White men, enabled White male professionals to solidify their relationships with each other while excluding their colleagues.[36]

For Black women, these gender-related cultural difficulties can be just as challenging as racial ones. Kelli, an attorney, recalled that she had begun her career expecting to encounter racial difficulties at her firm, but to her surprise had found that gender, not race, posed the significant problems: "It's rare that I do this, but I think gender plays a larger role on my team. . . . In terms of making those connections, the thing that limits the connections is gender. Because I don't want to talk about baseball. . . . When they're having 'locker-room' talks about women, locker-room talk about sports or whatever, they're not really talking about White people stuff—they're usually talking about men stuff." This banter shaped social activities away from the office, in which certain junior male colleagues connected with potential mentors and sponsors, while female professionals like Kelli were left on the outside looking in.[37] Kelli reported, "I've never been offered anything social because I've never talked to them about baseball or basketball or football." Such gendered exclusion can reflect some men's intent to exclude women, particularly from outings where men intend to speak or behave unprofessionally,[38] but in at least some instances it is likely a less intentional biproduct of homophily.

While further marginalizing Black women, these male-oriented cultural dynamics are a social lifeline for many Black men.[39] Several interviewees spoke of certain Black male professionals—in some instances, themselves—who used their interest in sports to gain entrance into powerful White-male-dominated networks at their firms. Brandon, who spoke about the importance of "commonalities" for building workplace social capital at his law firm, identified sports as a means of cultivating relationships with White male colleagues. He explained, "What helps with men, is [that] sports tends to be a universal language and they typically always unite around having an interest in sports." This was especially valuable for Brandon, who reported that "other than that [he] just didn't have a lot in common" with those colleagues. Similarly, James, who spoke of being unable to participate in his White colleagues' conversations about golf, partly overcome this disconnect by leveraging his knowledge about other sports and "talking basketball" with them.

Rooted in Racial Separateness

Social alienation ultimately stems from conditions outside of elite firms that shape the lives of Black and White professionals from childhood through their college and professional school years and into adulthood. Because of ongoing societal patterns of racial segregation and separateness, many Black and White professionals begin their careers with limited experience cultivating interracial friendships. Most White people reach adulthood with minimal social ties to Black people and little acclimation to their cultural and social preferences. As children, White Americans grow up in segregated neighborhoods and attend segregated schools. In college they make few close Black friends and seldom date or live with Black students or join majority-Black student groups.[40] As a result, most White adults do not know many Black people very well. A national survey found that the average White American has ninety-one White friends and only one Black friend.[41]

The converse is also true. Black Americans—including Black professionals—generally have limited prior social relationships with and acclimation to White people. This may seem surprising, as most Black professionals who join elite firms attended PWI colleges and universities, where they potentially enrolled in the same classes, ate in the same dining halls, and lived in the same dormitories as their future White colleagues. And as children, some also grew up in predominantly White towns and attended predominantly White schools, where they were in close physical proximity to many White peers and adults. But although they have been around White people and thrived—at least academically—in predominantly White institutions, many have led racially separate social lives in childhood, college, and professional school.

This racial separateness begins in childhood, thanks in part to persisting segregation in housing and education. Most White people grow up in White neighborhoods and attend White schools, with very few Black neighbors or classmates.[42] Meanwhile, most Black people grow up in Black neighborhoods, and nearly three-quarters of all Black students attend predominantly non-White schools.[43] This pattern spans the socioeconomic spectrum; Black middle-class families, although not as racially segregated as poor Black families, also disproportionately live in Black neighborhoods.[44] This segregation contributes to the shortage of interracial friendships, but it cannot explain all, or even most, of it. Researchers have found that the majority of the racial friendship gap remains even after statistically controlling for the effects of segregation.[45] Indeed, even Black students who attend predominantly White schools—including the elite private academies that serve as feeder schools to elite colleges—often end up with same-race friendship networks.[46]

These patterns grow stronger when students reach college, where they are evident across all types of personal relationships. Racial balkanization on university campuses—the tendency of students to socialize nearly exclusively with other members of their racial group—has been noted in academic research, student newspapers, and numerous firsthand accounts of life at elite colleges.[47] Even at elite PWIs, where Black students make up small percentages of the student body, many Black students' social and organizational lives are centered in their campuses' Black communities.[48] Black students at these schools usually join Black student organizations and join majority-White groups far less frequently.[49] Most have majority-Black social networks and few White friends.[50] These patterns grow increasingly pronounced over the course of students' collegiate careers. A longitudinal study in which researchers repeatedly surveyed students of one prestigious university about the composition of their friendship networks found that significantly more Black and White students reported having predominantly same-race social networks as seniors than they had three years earlier as freshmen.[51] Even greater racial separation exists in students' dating lives.[52] At some schools, these racialized social patterns become so deeply entrenched that they become normative to many Black students. Several interviewees who had socialized primarily with classmates from other racial groups in college reported that other Black students had seemed to regard them quizzically or even disapprovingly. Racial separateness also occurs at many professional schools.

These racialized social patterns have a variety of contributing factors. Many highly selective universities steer Black admitted students to special admitted students' weekends designed specifically for minority students, and several also offer racially themed residential housing.[53] These policies facilitate and therefore potentially increase racial separateness from when students first set foot on campus through the duration of their collegiate careers. Some interviewees described the impact of these policies in shaping their campus social lives. Maria, the attorney who reported that she had not made a single White friend in college or at her law firm,[54] attributed her racial isolation in part to her college's minority admissions program, which she claims steered her toward other minority students and away from her White future classmates. She explained that in contrast to the college's main program, which integrated admitted students into campus life, "for [the minority program] it was just, 'Oh come meet all the minority students.'" Maria felt that this separation ultimately disadvantaged Black attendees by limiting their integration into the broader campus community. Other interviewees voiced similar criticisms. Wesley, an attorney, spoke of a similar program at another Ivy League college. He complained, "They try and preach diversity at all these Ivy League schools, but when you get there they try to segregate the Black kids."

These university policies and programs are not the only—or even the primary—reason university students develop same-race networks. Segregated social patterns also arise because some Black students feel greater affinity toward other Black students and apprehension about their White classmates. A number of interviewees described finding their social homes within their school's "Black communities." Harold, an attorney, discussed finding a critical mass of Black students who sustained a "Black environment" at his Ivy League college. He described some of his college friends as having gone "through four years there and never interacted with

White people." Harold, who hailed from a majority-Black south-ern town, noted that he too spent most of his social and extracur-ricular life in college with his Black classmates. He explained, "I found . . . a large Black community of people a lot like myself, who shared a lot of the same interests, and who shared the same sense of humor. . . . I got involved with [a Black arts group] . . . And I pledged [a Black fraternity]." Other interviewees described similar patterns of racial separateness at their colleges. Two who attended another Ivy League college mentioned an area of their campus dining hall that Black students affectionately called "Little Africa," where many of them routinely congregated and ate. In describ-ing the extremely segregated patterns of student life at the highly ranked private institution that she attended for college, Demetria, a management consultant, recalled, "Everything was completely segregated. . . . If you weren't Black, I didn't know you."

As a result, many Black and White professionals develop diver-gent social and cultural preferences that ultimately render them less likely to form relationships and rapport with one another as adults. Deborah, whose problems fitting in at her law firm were discussed in the opening pages of this book, had attended almost exclusively Black and Latino elementary and junior high schools. There she developed social and cultural sensibilities that included a deep love for rap music and hip-hop culture. She then attended a predominantly White and Asian high school, where she devel-oped a core group of predominantly Black friends who shared her cultural interests. At her elite PWI she also immersed herself in the school's core Black community, holding leadership positions in multiple groups and engaging in campus activism on behalf of Black student interests. She had limited social experiences with her White classmates, and they were often awkward and nega-tive; she described multiple instances in which she was subjected to discomforting microaggressions and racially insensitive com-ments. It is not hard to understand how this social background, consisting of limited and often negative interactions with White peers, increased the risk that Deborah would encounter racial discomfort at her White law firm.

Other interviewees whose college lives were centered in their schools' Black communities also struggled at their firms. Agnes, an attorney, described immersing herself in Black social circles and organizations during her time attending an elite, predominantly White university: "If you looked at my photo albums from school, you would have thought that I went to Howard or Hampton or Spelman, because all my friends were Black. And we just had the community. . . . [A]ll your friends were Black, you were going to the Black mixers, the Kappa [Alpha Psi] parties, you were in the Black organizations. . . . My [college] experience—it was an HBCU experience, essentially." Agnes enjoyed her college experience, but her lack of interracial social engagement may have later limited her ability to develop social capital as a professional. At her firm Agnes established an extensive network of Black professionals, but she did not connect with White colleagues in her group and as a result struggled to access good assignments.

Clark, a former investment banker, described a similar set of experiences. Clark had grown up attending racially segregated, high-poverty urban public schools, where he had virtually no White classmates let alone friends. Although he had attended college at a predominantly White New England liberal arts college, the racial composition of his social network there resembled that of his childhood. "I lived in a Black dorm," Clark explained. "I probably stuck to the brothers and sisters [Black students] on the campus. I didn't really venture off too much unless you played basketball with me or something." Clark structured his personal life this way in part because he found the move from his underresourced urban high school to an affluent White liberal arts college very difficult. He noted, "I lived in an all-Black dorm for my first two years at the school. Because for me the transition was super hard. Academically, it was super hard. Socially, it was a little hard as well relating to White people." And when he began his career in investment banking, his limited interracial exposure worked to his disadvantage: "The one thing I would say that I missed out on in college is that the more interaction you have with White people, as a Black man coming from the kind of area where I came from, the better it prepares you to deal with them when you go into the working world. . . . That's what I figured out. . . . It was like, 'Fuck. This is weird. How do you relate to folks? How do you talk to folks the right way?'"

Greta, whose difficulties adapting to the social and cultural terrain of her Wall Street firm were previously noted, traced her discomfort and displeasure with her White colleagues' end-of-the-week get-togethers to racially informed differences in the social and cultural preferences they developed in college. Greta had attended affluent, predominantly White schools, where she had socialized almost exclusively with other Black students, who engaged in social activities different from those of their White peers. She explained, "We [Black people] don't play beer pong, and beer games and 'flippy-cup' and all these other things in college. . . . There's a socialization that happens in college that is different from one culture to another. And if you don't know and have never been socialized in that way, you go into the corporate setting where there's people who already have something familiar happening and the cliques start happening, just naturally, and you get excluded from things and you have to encourage yourself to go. And that's one thing we fail to do."

As Greta observed, the cultural milieus of these groups often reflect experiences and preferences that their White counterparts had cultivated many years earlier. Aja, an associate at a major southern law firm, drew similar conclusions after observing that her White colleagues regularly socialized with each other by "grabbing a couple beers" at nearby bars. Aja explained that while these types of outings were consistent with the practices that she had observed among her White classmates in college and law school, they differed from those of many Black professionals, including herself: "I mean, I started drinking beer when I got to the firm so that I could be social. I didn't drink beer in college, you know. If we drank, we drank liquor, but [Black] girls just didn't drink beer. Black girls drink a hell of a lot less beer than White girls do. And it was just different socially."

Sylvester, an investment banker, offered a similar perspective, but in less gendered terms, explaining matter-of-factly, "[We] weren't going to bars and hanging out and drinking beer. We went to clubs—*Black clubs* that played *our* music." These differences affected his transition to the firm. Sylvester found that to build rapport with his colleagues, most of whom were White, he needed to acclimate himself to their nightlife tastes and adjust to their social rituals, including drinking sessions at White bars. This did not come naturally for him. "So there was a little bit of a learning curve on getting up to speed and comfortable with that," he explained. Greta's, Aja's, and Sylvester's observations linking college to workplace social dynamics are consistent with the observations of scholars who have researched college life. As sociologists Elizabeth Armstrong and Laura Hamilton have noted, people develop and solidify lasting "cultural tastes" and "social styles" in college,[55] and they carry these traits into adulthood.

The Intersection of Race and Class

Race and gender are not solely responsible for the cultural alienation Black professionals experience at elite firms. These difficulties often also reflect class-based differences. For example, although James, the attorney, spoke about not playing golf while growing up as a racial difference, golf participation also varies by social class. As James grew up in near-poverty, the fact that he played basketball instead of golf in his youth has both racial and class-based dimensions. Several interviewees reported that colleagues seemed to privilege certain cultural traits associated with high socioeconomic status. This tendency disadvantages many Black professionals, who seldom hail from such backgrounds—particularly early in their careers, when they have had limited exposure to more affluent lifestyles. Brandon sensed that his family's social class background left him without some of the cultural resources taken for granted by attorneys at his firm: "Being introduced to a law firm environment, you go to places and there's a wine list and they sit down and pick wines, and I didn't know much about that—[my family] didn't even drink wine. . . . They ask, 'Where did you summer?' I didn't summer anywhere—I'm from a middle-class family. My folks stayed in [my hometown] so I went home when I had breaks." He explained that these dynamics created social boundaries that impeded Black associates from bonding with senior colleagues: "I think that's the sort of commonality of experience that there's just no substitute for. I didn't come from that world; I didn't have a whole lot in common with them. I didn't appreciate the same sorts of things. . . . I think that's part of what keeps you from developing the mentoring relationships."

As Brandon made clear in distinguishing his "middle-class" upbringing from his colleagues' more affluent backgrounds, class-based differences can work closely with racial differences to alienate Black professionals. This is not always the case, however. In some instances, these class-based dynamics actually benefit Black professionals from more privileged backgrounds, who have more of the cultural capital valued at their firms. This was not lost on Brandon. Referring to a well-known Black author who hailed from an affluent background, he surmised, "I'm sure you'd probably get a different answer from the 'Lawrence Otis Graham kids' . . . the kids who went to Groton and come from wealthy backgrounds."[56]

These interviewees' descriptions of class-based cultural schema at their firms are consistent with research demonstrating that elite institutions often reward people who possess cultural traits associated with higher social class backgrounds.[57] In *Pedigree*, Rivera observed that job seekers who possessed certain cultural traits more common among people from affluent backgrounds were the main beneficiaries of cultural matching in hiring.[58] Sociologists Sam Friedman and Daniel Laurison also found that employers privilege the cultural traits of workers from affluent backgrounds in ways that materially advantage them over their colleagues from more humble origins.

Leondra, who previously worked at a major Wall Street investment bank, suffered a number of difficulties that she attributed to her class background. Leondra had grown up in a very poor inner-city neighborhood, and as most of the students she befriended at her Ivy League college were also students of color from working-class and poor families, she began her job with very little exposure to the unwritten cultural norms of her bank. "I didn't know how to act in the corporate environment," she explained. "There are certain rules that you have to follow, such as how you dress, . . . what you eat, the things you watch on TV, the music you listen to." Unfamiliar with these cultural preferences, Leondra engaged in conduct that marked her as an outsider and drew adverse judgments from her colleagues. Gloria, an attorney, also recalled experiencing intense class-based discomfort early in her legal career. Although Gloria comes across as an outgoing, confident, and assertive person, the socioeconomic tilt of workplace conversations undermined her self-confidence and made her reluctant to interact with her colleagues socially: "I remember feeling uncomfortable sometimes at lunches—like my first lunch when they were talking about Gucci bags and Fendi bags. . . . I love handbags but I couldn't even fathom spending a thousand dollars on a purse. . . . I remember they'd be talking about 'Oh, I flew over to Italy this weekend,' and I [couldn't] even wrap my mind around having that kind of money. Or even doing that even if I had that kind of money."

Although Gloria would soon have enough income to pay for expensive handbags and trips to Europe, she found the fact that her peers already were accustomed to such lifestyles disorienting. "I don't know what to do when I'm in that situation," she said. "I kind of just disappear and they take me under their wing like I'm their poor little puppy." This social dynamic made her feel like an outsider who was not on equal footing with her colleagues.

Nearly a decade later, Gloria still encountered class-related difficulties in her interactions with colleagues. Although she now better understood her rich colleagues' tastes, she still resented the constant class-based skew of their conversations. Gloria complained, "I have a hard time still, because at some point it gets monotonous. You know, [it's] the same shit. I don't give a fuck about your golf outing—I don't care, I don't care. I don't give a fuck about your summer home—I don't care about none of that shit." Gloria's lack of familiarity with—or interest in—her colleagues' lifestyles rendered her interactions with them laborious and unenjoyable, contributing to her alienation. "It's certainly a game you have to play [. . .] but I don't enjoy it," she explained. "I have to be in a certain mood."

Conclusion

Social alienation is the joint product of racial conditions within and beyond these firms. The racial separateness prevalent throughout America, the predominantly White racial composition of elite firms, and the universal tendency of cultural homophily all conspire to disadvantage many Black professionals. They do so chiefly by making it more difficult for Black professionals to develop social capital, thereby depriving them of access to various resources, opportunities, and rewards. That this dynamic is cultural in nature and not necessarily the result of racial bias does not make it any less problematic or consequential. These disadvantages are still critical impediments to firms' efforts to achieve fairer, more inclusive workplaces.

4

Why Some Black Professionals Thrive

Not all Black professionals who work at elite firms have bad experiences there. Although they remain heavily underrepresented, thousands of Black professionals now hold partnership-level positions in America's largest law firms, investment banks, and management consulting firms. Some of my respondents had achieved highly successful careers at their firms. Beth was a partner at one of the most prestigious law firms in the country, and Sandra and Rachel were well on their way to becoming partners at theirs. Other interviewees had led successful careers at their firms before moving to prestigious positions in government, private equity, or in-house with major clients. Many of these interviewees raved about their experiences at their firms, which is perhaps unsurprising given their triumphant careers and the support and accolades they had received from colleagues. But other interviewees whose careers had been less distinguished expressed similar views.

These interviewees' experiences raise important questions: How and why do some Black professionals enjoy positive experiences in firms that are inhospitable to others? How are some able to forge close relationships with colleagues while others toil in isolation? There is no single answer, as a number of factors can contribute to one Black professional's having a better career than others. Perhaps most obviously, the quality of their work performance matters. Natalie, a management consultant who earned multiple promotions at her firm, emphasized that performing well on assignments was critical for developing sponsors: "The biggest, biggest, biggest, biggest, biggest nugget there is that you have to have a good track record. No one's gonna go to bat for you if you don't have a good track record. . . . Even if they believe in diversity, even if they believe in bringing the right people up. They're not going to go to bat for you if they know that you don't have a certain performance." Some professionals are better able than others to reach this high performance level. Their ability to do so varies according to a number of attributes, including their analytical abilities, writing skills, attention to detail, and drive. All other things being equal, professionals who are stronger in these areas should have an easier time outperforming their peers and impressing their senior colleagues.

Sheer chance also plays a role.[1] Through completely fortuitous circumstances, some professionals luck into valuable opportunities and meet generous mentors and sponsors early in their careers, while others receive assignments working with senior colleagues who are unhelpful and unfair. Sandra, the attorney, attributed her beneficial relationships with powerful sponsors at her firm in part to her good fortune in being assigned to work with especially supportive partners. "I just think that I got lucky," she explained. She contrasted her experience with those of Black associates who were assigned to work with less supportive partners: "Let's put it this way: I certainly know other associates of color at the firm who work hard and haven't had the same kind of payoff. . . . Some partners are just like 'write me the brief and I don't really care about you after you're done.' And if they've worked with people like that, then that really can hinder your development and who you're exposed to and the type of cases you get." Luke, an attorney, recalled what he described as a "fluke" occurrence in which he came to work "uncharacteristically early one morning" and an influential partner looking for help with an urgent task stopped by his office. Luke aced the assignment, and the partner, pleased with his work, then staffed Luke on other high-profile matters that enabled him to develop his skills and reputation. Other interviewees also shared stories of fortuitous opportunities and encounters that had changed the course of their careers.

Differences in firm-level and departmental conditions beyond Black professionals' control also impact their careers in ways that can lead to some enjoying better outcomes than others. Black professionals hired into especially busy and thinly staffed departments may face less risk of discrimination because their colleagues may need to work with them by necessity due to a shortage of other available professionals. Caitlin, an attorney, received more substantive responsibilities and greater client contact than many of her peers because of her good fortune in being assigned to a very small practice group. Similarly, LaTonya, a midlevel associate at another large law firm, sensed that the lean organizational structure of her small department may have helped her career by limiting her senior colleagues' discretion to discriminate against her: "I just got the impression that there was work that needed to be done, and everyone was looking at the bottom line, and they wanted to give it to the person who could do it right, and who could do it fast. . . . It's not like they were looking at all these choices—that they were looking at these 15 White guys and me. They really didn't have the opportunity to pass over me for good work." Although LaTonya had begun making plans to pursue a nonlegal career and described herself as "not a big fan of this place" and "not invested," she nonetheless reported that she had been treated fairly at her firm: "I felt that there was no race or gender bias, and I would be the first person to point it out if I thought it was there." As Caitlin's and LaTonya's accounts suggest, having the good fortune to work in thinly staffed departments can potentially enhance Black professionals' career prospects substantially.[2]

Thus, although the impact of chance on career outcomes is difficult to measure and often ignored, such vagaries can send professionals onto divergent trajectories just as surely as differences in talent and performance can.[3] In attempting to understand why some Black professionals fail while others succeed, it is therefore important to recognize that not all differences in outcomes can be explained by merit or by social processes such as racial discrimination or discomfort.

Relationships with White Sponsors

A common thread in the accounts of the most successful interviewees and others who were highly satisfied with their careers is that almost to a person they each identified senior White male professionals in their firms who had advanced their careers by providing them with crucial opportunities, advocacy, and advice. They regarded these mentors and sponsors as critical to their career outcomes. Beth described the many ways that her chief sponsor—whom she described as "a middle-aged White Republican guy"—had championed her career, ultimately enabling her to make partner: "He got me put on different committees in the legal community in the city. He taught me how to think about myself as business and how to build my brand. He made sure I didn't work with certain people who were absolutely nasty . . . he also worked to keep me on matters where I was getting exposed to the right people." Similarly, Sandra described how her sponsors had steered valuable developmental opportunities her way, both directly—by pulling her onto their cases—and indirectly, by praising her to other partners.

When I came in the door, I got with some partners who were just really good about saying, "You were great, I'm going to recommend that so-and-so works with you" or "Here's another case for you to work on." Who were just really good about that. And I know that everybody certainly isn't like that. I just feel that I got lucky. . . . [The head of the department] has sort of taken an interest in me. She's got me on my last three cases just by making calls and saying "Hey, [Sandra] should be on this case."

Some Black professionals also benefited from their relationships with sponsors more indirectly. Donna, an attorney, explained that because of her close relationship with the head of her department, she enjoyed "a certain amount of protection," in that some of the more difficult attorneys in the department "tread a little more lightly and are a little more careful in how free they feel to be abusive" toward her, a phenomenon that social scientists refer to as "reflected power."[*] This power also emboldened Donna to decline certain grunt work assignments so that she could focus on premium assignments more beneficial to her career. She reported that as a result she had a "good professional experience" despite working in a department that was known as being "hostile to Black associates."

In these and other ways, relationships with sponsors can greatly benefit Black professionals by increasing both their access to career capital and their subjective satisfaction with their experiences at their firms.

Interactional Ease

There are many reasons some Black professionals end up with more sponsors than others. In addition to pure chance and their performance on assignments, another trait also plays a critical role: their comfort when interacting with White people in White-dominated settings. Black professionals who possess this comfort are better able to use informal interactions with senior colleagues—such as conversations during chance hallway encounters or visits to their offices to make small talk—to increase their access to career capital. At her firm, Sandra regularly contacted senior White colleagues to seek both mentorship and work opportunities (outside of the firm's formal assignment process). She explained, "I really did seek people out to go to lunch, I really did just stop by partners' offices and be like 'Hey, I heard you're working on this case. I think that's really interesting. Do you need help?'" Sandra sensed that these efforts advantaged her over Black colleagues who seemed surprised by her tactics and less comfortable engaging in this kind of networking: "When I shared with [Black] junior associates that I really did go by so-and-so's office and say, 'Hey, I saw this on the new business matter list, do you need help?' they looked at me like I was crazy. The associates were like 'Oh my god, you did that?' But I honestly feel like that's what a lot of the White people do." Sandra considered this strategy of reaching out to White colleagues for mentorship and assignments critical to her success. She explained, "I think that helped me a lot, and I think it's something that actually Black associates don't do."

Sandra was not the only interviewee who profited from engaging senior White colleagues in personal interactions. Rachel described how her persistent efforts to solicit work from a powerful White partner eventually bore fruit and changed the trajectory of her career: "I would go up to him and say, 'Hi, Mr. [Partner's last name]. I'm a new associate, I'm looking for work, I'm in the . . . office over there if you need me.' And so I did that enough that when something came up, he asked me to do it. We had a client [with an urgent legal problem] so I wrote up a memo on it, and he was immediately impressed." This sequence of events helped propel Rachel onto her firm's partnership track. The partner became a key sponsor, giving her sophisticated assignments on high-profile matters and encouraging other partners to do the same. As Rachel continued to perform superlatively on each successive assignment, her reputation and skill set grew. She believed that her comfort at initiating interactions with senior White professionals like this partner advantaged her over many other Black professionals. Her ability to perform stellar work was also important, but if she had not been willing to repeatedly solicit additional opportunities and able to engage her senior White male colleagues in easy banter, her career might have unfolded quite differently, ultimately causing her to miss out on millions of dollars in lifetime earnings. Natalie, the consultant, also described working proactively to initiate interactions and develop relationships with powerful senior White colleagues: "It was being strategic—I had to be tactical. . . . I would often go and talk to the person and say 'Oh, I heard that you have this article that's coming up, and I would be happy to give you research.' I would always send holiday cards. I knew their wives' and their children's birthdays, so I would say, 'Tell your wife I said happy birthday.'" Natalie credited these efforts with enabling her to accrue "a lot of champions" and "a lot of mentors." Beth, the law firm partner, confirmed the importance of these outreach efforts by reflecting on her own mentoring practices: "The reality of it is—I need people who want to be mentored by me to come to me. And the people who get the best of my mentoring are the people who are the best about seeking me out. I can't seek out every person in the firm to give advice because I have a practice of my own to run."

The most successful interviewees also exhibited ease around their White colleagues in other ways. They appeared less likely to engage in the self-concealment behavior that other Black professionals with more stigma anxiety used.[5] Some took pride in refusing to use such covering strategies. Beth, describing herself and the other Black partner in her department, said, "We're both *very*

Black people. We take pride in being Black, and there's nobody in the firm who would think otherwise." Similarly, Rachel insisted, "I'm the same person in my office, at the firm, at home—I don't have different personas." Although Rachel had the cultural capital to engage with her White colleagues on their preferred terms when she so chose, she did not attempt to hide other cultural traits that reflected her Blackness. She asserted, "I'm the last person to say 'Oh, you need to be like a White person.' Because I really love who I am and my heritage." In fact, Rachel at times revealed information about herself that likely rendered her racial identity more salient; for example, during one outing with members of her work group she demonstrated her knowledge about basketball and shared with her colleagues that she had social ties with a Black professional athlete. Rachel also discussed Black popular culture with her colleagues. She explained, "They'll . . . say [Rachel], 'I'm sure you know about Jay-Z,' and I don't feel bad saying, 'Yeah, I do.'" While many Black professionals quite reasonably would have felt uncomfortable navigating these types of racially loaded conversations while at work, Rachel's interactional ease insulated her from any such potential embarrassment or resentment. In doing so, it better enabled her to build social capital with her White colleagues.

Beth, who criticized other Black attorneys for their workplace reticence,[6] took pride in her own refusal to self-silence and made clear that she was not at all concerned about being stereotyped as an "angry Black woman." She explained, "My outlook is . . . if someone treats me in an unfair manner, they're getting cursed out. I'm not taking that. And I think that's apparent in my demeanor. I came to do a job." Sandra's, Rachel's, and Beth's accounts reveal that some of the prevailing descriptions that present Black professional life as a monolith of discomfort and despair are overly broad.[7] Although Black women are underrepresented in positions of power and potentially disadvantaged on the basis of both race and gender, these interviewees all were quite comfortable and successful at their firms.

Star performers are not the only Black professionals who benefit from interactional ease. Other interviewees who did not achieve similar levels of career success at their firms nonetheless also seemed to gain advantages from the ease with which they interacted with White colleagues. Regina, a consultant, emphasized that she made a point *not* to self-conceal during conversations with White colleagues because she believed that she could better build rapport with them by sharing her authentic personality and sense of humor. "Significant differences in the way you carry yourself or how you interact with people . . . I just don't do that," she explained. "I'm really myself. . . . I don't think about, 'Oh, these are my White colleagues, I can't say that in front of them.'" Regina described how her unfiltered conversational style helped her build close rapport and camaraderie with one White partner who—to the surprise of some of their colleagues—eventually adopted some of her slang. Regina reflected on this: "Maybe people wouldn't approve. Like maybe they would be like, 'you shouldn't do that in front of the White partner blah blah blah,' but I believe that in a way, that's breaking down barriers."

Jack, an attorney who described his work performance as unexceptional, nonetheless acquired useful career capital by socializing with his colleagues away from the office. As a result, he fared far better at the firm than he would have on the basis of his performance alone. Jack reported that his membership in his group's after-work-drinks crew resulted in his receiving better treatment than certain peers who outperformed him on their assignments. He noted, "I saw people who did good work, but never went out, and they were not as connected and did not have as good of a time. . . . I did *good* work but because I went out, I had a *great* time there. A great time." In one instance Jack was able to leverage a social relationship he had formed with a senior colleague over drinks to his professional advantage. Jack, then a junior associate, approached a partner he had befriended through these outings and proposed an ambitious business development trip to another continent. This venture proved successful; it netted the partner an important client and raised Jack's profile at the firm. Although this was only a minor victory in the grand scheme of things—Jack did not have a particularly distinguished career at the firm and left within a few years—his experience illustrates how Black professionals comfortable in racial isolation may enjoy greater access to career capital and other advantages that make their time at their firms more fruitful and enjoyable.

This interactional ease in White social spaces can also help Black professionals overcome cultural differences to forge relationships with White colleagues. Quincy provided an example of this when he described attending professional hockey games on outings spearheaded by a partner in his department. All of the associates in his group received invitations to these games, but some were better able than others to take advantage of these opportunities. As few Black people follow hockey, a sport with a famously White fan base, these events were not very popular with Quincy's Black colleagues:[8] "Lots of times they'll send out emails saying, 'We're gonna go to a hockey game. Partner X wants to invite you to the firm suite for a hockey game. Who's interested?' A lot of [Black] people are like, 'Hockey? I hate hockey. Why would I go do that?'" In contrast, Quincy was more inclined to attend these events and comfortable enough to attempt to overcome his lack of interest in the sport, in order to optimize his career. As he described his approach to these social opportunities, "The person who's the biggest go-getter is like, 'I do hate hockey, I would rather do anything other than watch hockey tonight, but Partner X is going to be there so I need to go. I need to go smile and shake hands and talk about hockey like I know what I'm talking about or just let him talk about hockey and just listen and smile and nod.'"

For Black professionals, these informal outings can be sites of labor instead of leisure. At these hockey games Quincy had to work to overcome his cultural alienation, while White associates who enjoyed hockey were able to bond through authentic, well-informed conversations about the game. But notwithstanding his disadvantage relative to his White peers, his prior experiences in White-dominated settings likely made this undertaking far less daunting for him than for many of his Black peers, who generally opted not to attend.

White Familiarity

The ease that certain Black professionals enjoy in these interactions is not just a reflection of their personality or social skills. Rather, it also stems from their prior social interactions and relationships with other White people in other White spaces. Just as the many Black professionals who arrive at these firms with limited or negative interracial experiences may be especially likely to experience social alienation or stigma anxiety on the job, Black professionals who have more positive and extensive prior interactions may experience greater ease.[9] For those with these prior experiences, being the only Black professional on a work team or at an office happy hour is a fundamentally different, and less difficult, experience than it is for other Black professionals. Having spent hundreds—or even thousands—of hours with White friends, dating partners, and family members over the course of their lives, in White-dominated settings, they begin their careers well accustomed to conditions of racial isolation and forming rapport across racial lines. As a result, they find their firms less racially threatening. Their prior experiences also help them professionally by giving them access to the cultural traits that carry currency among their White colleagues. Because of this exposure, some of them actually benefit from cultural homophily, the dynamic that disadvantages so many other Black professionals.

This experience-based comfort can perhaps best be described as *White familiarity*. White familiarity is an example of what sociologist Pierre Bourdieu has termed *habitus*, a broad-ranging construct that encompasses the habits, attitudes, beliefs, self-presentation styles, and social skills that people draw from as they move through life.[10] Habitus like White familiarity is shaped by people's past experiences, which in turn shape how people interpret their current situations and develop expectations about future ones. Habitus informs how people navigate their surroundings in pursuing their personal and professional goals and determines whether individuals perceive particular tactics to be useful or counterproductive, reasonable or reckless.[11] Although one's habitus is shaped by broad social identity traits such as race and class,[12] habitus also differs within identity groups according to people's individual life experiences. Accordingly, depending on their prior interracial relationships and interactions, individual Black professionals begin their careers with very different dispositions and expectations concerning their firms and their White colleagues.

COMFORT AT WHITE FIRMS

The interviewees who reported the most positive experiences at their firms generally had begun their careers possessing White familiarity. Several posited that because their life experiences had accustomed them to conditions of racial isolation, they did not find their firms' racial demographics disadvantageous or daunting. Beth explained that as a child she had attended an affluent, predominantly White private school where she had a great experience with White teachers she described as "very encouraging" and "very meritocratic." Beth then attended college and law school at Ivy League universities, where she enjoyed supportive relationships with a number of professors and distinguished herself academically. Reflecting back on these earlier experiences, Beth posited that they likely made her more comfortable at her firm: "I've never felt that [out of place at the firm] because I've always been in all-White, privileged environments. That's what I was accustomed to. So this place didn't feel any more distressing to me than any other thing I had dealt with previously. I never got the sense that the law firm wasn't my firm every bit as much as it was the White guy's next to me."

Derrick, a consultant, attributed the ease that he felt as one of very few Black consultants in his entire office to his intensively interracial personal background. For much of his childhood Derrick had attended schools with relatively few Black students, and he had participated in and formed friendships through a number of predominantly White student activities, such as fencing. Most of his friends at the Ivy League college he attended were also non-Black. Derrick shared that as a result of these interracial relationships and those he continued to have as an adult, he did not experience any alienation or anxiety at his firm. He explained, "I'm used to it. 95% of the time, that's me. That speaks to the circles I'm in, socially, professionally, the extracurricular activities, et cetera, where it's to the point that I just don't notice it. I take note of it, but it doesn't really change how I operate."

Quincy, the attorney who begrudgingly accompanied his White colleagues on office hockey outings, had attended affluent White schools from childhood through law school. He sensed that his interactions and relationships with White educators, coaches, and classmates' parents at these institutions gave him advantages over other Black professionals. Quincy explained that unlike some of his Black colleagues, "I personally have grown *very* comfortable dealing with White authority figures because I've been dealing with them my entire life. So it's not difficult for me at all. I also grew in a predominantly Jewish neighborhood in [a major city] so . . . I'm also used to dealing with older White Jewish authority figures, which is definitely something you have to deal with at a New York City law firm. So I don't feel that uncomfortable at all really."

Wayne, who resented having to conform to his colleagues' cultural preferences to network with them at office social events and outings,[13] nonetheless was able to do so effectively because he had attended affluent, predominantly White schools since childhood and was used to socializing in White spaces (many of his closest friends were White). He explained that fitting in at his firm "wasn't really a problem, because I've pretty much been operating in these environments for most of my life. It didn't feel any different than anywhere else I've ever been—it wasn't, 'Holy shit, this is a culture shock—I need to adapt!'" Although he disapproved of being forced to conform to the skewed cultural dynamics of his office, his White familiarity made his office interactions and outings less difficult than they otherwise would have been. Regina also sensed that her prior interracial background—which entailed good relationships with White friends, teachers, and family members—"created some level of comfort" for her at her large management consulting firm.

Other interviewees who were comfortable at their firms shared similar information about their backgrounds. Growing up, Sandra had flourished socially and academically in a predominantly White community where most of her friends had been White.[14] Rachel also had thrived despite being the only Black child in most of her classes in the predominantly White town where she had been raised. She also had great interracial experiences at the PWI she attended for college, where she was a prominent student leader and highly involved in non-Black student organizations. Henry, the attorney who landed an in-house position with a prestigious client,[15] had been class president at his majority-White high school. In college and as a young adult he had participated in a number of predominantly White activities and organizations, studied abroad in Europe, and even played in a rock band. He shared that many of his closest friends were White.

The accounts of these Black professionals illustrate some of the subtle advantages of interracial immersion during their formative years. This process resembles that which sociologist Anthony Jack observed in his research on a different type of elite institution, a highly selective university.[16] In *The Privileged Poor*, Jack noticed that some socioeconomically disadvantaged minority students had previously acclimated themselves to the cultural traits common among their White college peers while attending elite prep schools. He labeled this group "the privileged poor" and found that its members were more comfortable at their universities, and enjoyed a greater sense of belonging, than other low-income minority students.[17] Jack attributed these differences to their greater familiarity with the consumption practices and cultural traits of their rich classmates.[18] As with Jack's privileged poor, some Black professionals also benefit from the cultural resources and comfort that they attain through prior exposure and experiences in other White settings.

Black professionals recognized these potential advantages even when they did not benefit from them firsthand. Several interviewees described friends and colleagues who appeared to profit from White familiarity. Harold, an attorney, began his career with limited interracial exposure, having grown up in a predominantly Black southern town and immersed himself in his school's "Black community" in college. He sensed that this background put him at a disadvantage against Black professionals from more racially integrated circumstances. He discussed one such person in particular—a close friend and former law school classmate—whose background growing up in a more diverse city and attending schools with more White classmates and friends may have helped her surpass him professionally.

> Whereas we were doing the same in law school, and I even had an easier time getting a job . . . she excelled and just did really, really well [at her firm]. . . . I always attribute the difference to being [that] she knows how to get along better with those sort[s] of people who are decisionmakers. Her ability to work with older White men was much better than my ability to work with older White men, and it had huge differences in how she was perceived and how work went for her . . . that's something that comes a little easier for [her]—she'll go out to drink with a partner from her law firm.

While Harold floated between multiple firms, struggling at each, this friend eventually made partner at hers.

Consistent with Harold's account, Clark observed that at his former investment bank, Black professionals who had previously interacted more extensively with White people fared better than Black professionals who had not. He asserted, "I've noticed that if you have experiences where you've been engaged with a lot of White folks early on in your life, in certain companies you do very, very well." Clark's claim is a bit of an overgeneralization; not all Black professionals with early interracial interactions do "very, very well" at these firms. But the general pattern he identified is consistent with other interviewees' accounts.

POSSIBLE SIGNIFICANCE OF FAMILY BACKGROUNDS

The likelihood of Black professionals' having White familiarity may depend upon their family backgrounds, particularly their social class and national origins. Black Americans raised in poor households have especially limited opportunities for interracial immersion, as they are even more likely than other Black people to grow up in segregated communities and to attend predominantly non-White schools.[19] As a result, in college they may be especially likely to gravitate toward students from similar backgrounds. In contrast, children from more affluent Black families have more opportunities for interracial relationships and greater exposure to White cultural traits due to their somewhat greater propinquity to White children in their classrooms and neighborhoods.[20] Similarly, Black professionals from immigrant families also have greater opportunities to develop in-depth interracial relationships as children, as they live and attend school with more White peers and report weaker feelings of racial group identity.[21] For these and other reasons, they may be less likely to experience stigma anxiety and alienation as professionals.[22]

Limitations and Potential Drawbacks

Although White familiarity can be an important resource, it is difficult to measure or prove its impact. White familiarity works in conjunction with various other traits, including talent, luck, ambition, shrewdness, and sociability. When a Black professional succeeds at an elite firm, there is no way to measure how much each of these different traits is responsible. White familiarity does not invariably lead to career success; some Black professionals who possess it still have negative experiences. This is not surprising, as many professionals of all races are unhappy at these firms, and most only last for a few years.[23] White familiarity also does not shield Black professionals from discrimination. Black professionals who work with racist, unfair, or unsupportive colleagues may suffer adverse outcomes regardless of how comfortable they are interacting with White people in White-dominated spaces.

Furthermore, White familiarity may prevent Black professionals from recognizing, addressing, or avoiding unfair treatment. Black professionals who have had positive prior experiences in White institutions and social settings may underestimate the racial risks at their firms and therefore fail to take suitable precautions against them. Nonetheless, the experiences of my interviewees suggest that White familiarity is a valuable resource that insulates Black professionals from the disadvantages of racial discomfort.

Perspectives on the Significance of Race

In general, the Black professionals who were most satisfied with their careers described the racial climates of their firms very differently than other interviewees and Black professionals in other studies. Some downplayed the significance of race at their firms altogether, offering views that contained elements of what some sociologists have labeled "colorblind racism."[24] They described their firms as meritocratic institutions where discrimination was rare because racial biases were trumped by senior professionals' desire to maximize profits. Beth, for example, maintained that her firm was simply "too busy" and focused on preserving its reputation for excellence to discriminate against high-performing attorneys. She claimed, "The culture is that when it comes down to the business and making money, they just want the best person for the job."

Some of these interviewees brought up examples of individual Black professionals who had succeeded at their firms as "proof" of the limited impact of race there. In describing the large law firm where he began his career, Jack noted that two of the partners in his group were Black, including one who had just recently made partner. He interpreted this information as proving the irrelevance of race at the firm, concluding that "there wasn't anything that could hold you back or anything that could be considered some kind of racial barrier or anything." Oscar, an attorney, came to sense that race was a relatively insignificant barrier at his firm, based on both the success of his mentor, a Black partner, and his own positive experiences there: "I *do* think that race might be a little overplayed. Because I really do believe, and I really have encountered, that if you do good work—it's not always the case, but if you really, really do good work—that that's gonna be valued no matter what your race is. . . . Because that's been my experience, personally."

Beth's, Jack's, and Oscar's views about the limited impact of race, though in tension with the extensive body of research and reporting documenting disparities and perceptions of discrimination at these firms, are far from unique. Other interviewees downplayed the significance of race at their firms by emphasizing that large professional services firms were difficult places for professionals of all races. Several described the plight of certain White colleagues to demonstrate that problems often characterized as race specific actually were, in their opinions, universal.[25] For them, arbitrary, potentially unfair outcomes were simply "the nature of the beast" or "luck of the draw" at these firms. Joshua, a former investment banker, observed that highly qualified White bankers were regularly denied promotions at his bank because of an oversupply of talented young professionals relative to the number of senior positions available. He explained, "There are a lot of intelligent, hardworking White men who just didn't get promoted to managing director or didn't get promoted to partner—not because they're White or because of whatever else, but because it's a tough, competitive place." Joshua used this observation to express skepticism about whether discrimination was afoot when impressive Black bankers were denied promotion: "You see the people who are promoted from VP to MD, and every year ten people who probably could have made it, didn't. . . . [If] there was a Black person in that group, they couldn't say that, 'ok, it was because

I'm Black,' because there were ten White guys who were equally competent, and they didn't get the opportunity either.'"

Joshua expanded upon this post-racial perspective by criticizing some of his Black colleagues for complaining about racial isolation in their departments. Dismissing their concerns, Joshua stated, "Many times people will say, 'Oh, I'm the only African American.' And I'll go, 'This other guy's the only Pakistani, this other guy's the only guy from Ireland, this other guy's the only guy from India,' so you really can't use excuses or crutches to kind of push along."

In attempting to refute his colleagues' concerns, Joshua engaged in a logical fallacy of false equivalence by ignoring obvious differences in the racial stereotypes that affect the members of different racial groups and leave some at higher risk of discrimination. Joshua's perspective downplaying racial disadvantages at his firm was likely shaped by his prior life experiences. As a child he had attended predominantly White schools where he felt respected and embraced by White teachers and classmates (who voted him class president) alike. These early experiences may have instilled in Joshua an enduring skepticism about the relevance of race.

Harmony, a successful attorney, used similar logic to downplay the significance of race at her firm. She emphasized that some attorneys of all races suffer outcomes unrelated to their deservingness or their demonstrated work capabilities and concluded that the misfortunes of individual Black professionals presumably also are seldom related to race: "I [work with] White first-year associates who might not have gotten hooked up with the right people when they got here . . . and now it's very likely that they may get fired. So it has nothing to do with [race]; to me it's a universal problem." Harmony makes an important observation, but she also makes a logical leap in denying the possible impact of race. For although she is right that associates of all races face risks and negative outcomes at these firms, race still can render some attorneys more vulnerable than others. Jonah, an attorney, also downplayed the impact of race at his firm by emphasizing the misfortunes of White colleagues. To refute what he considered an undue tendency to infer racial discrimination when Black attorneys suffered adverse outcomes, Jonah described one particular incident in which a well-regarded White attorney was seemingly inexplicably terminated. In referring to the White attorney he posited that "most of us would have believed it was discrimination if it was a Black man." Jonah insisted that many observers—including his Black colleagues—overestimated the role of racism in the negative career outcomes of Black attorneys at his firm. He asserted that "the fact of the matter is, it's not always race."

Jonah and several other interviewees also attributed persisting disparities at their firms to alleged shortcomings of Black professionals. Jonah criticized some of his Black peers for, in his view, not understanding the unwritten "rules of the game" for junior professionals at elite firms. While he prided himself on being shrewd at managing departmental politics and maneuvering to access the right work with the right partners, he disparagingly claimed that "the other Black people don't know what they're doing." Other interviewees—including Beth, the law firm partner who faulted Black female attorneys for undermining their own careers—blamed Black professionals for their own stigma anxieties.

Harmony, who made (nonequity) partner at her firm shortly after our interview, explained that in her opinion, "anybody who comes to a law firm and has the ability to do good work and makes a cognizant effort to do all the things that you need to succeed at a law firm, will." Harmony insisted that the disparities in attrition and promotions at her firm reflected racial differences in career aspirations. She asserted, "I don't think a lot of Black people come to law firms wanting to be successful. They want to make good money and leave after a few years." Although Harmony was not the only interviewee to express the view that fewer Black professionals aspire to rise through the ranks at elite firms, several others rejected this idea. They posited instead that any such differences in career plans likely stemmed from Black professionals perceiving that they would not receive fair opportunities to advance at their firms.

Other successful professionals offered more nuanced accounts of the role of race. Sandra, despite her own positive experiences, reported that Black associates needed to "stand out" and perform impeccably on assignments to earn access to the kinds of opportunities and reputational capital that less impressive White associates receive as a matter of course: "I don't think we can be average and sail through and still get good opportunities like a lot of the White kids can. I really do think that we have to work harder. . . . [If] you don't go the extra mile and you're a Black associate, it can be to your detriment." Sandra was able to overcome this double standard, but she believed that it created an "uphill battle" for Black professionals. Nonetheless, Sandra and other interviewees suggested that race could even be a net positive for some Black professionals because certain senior colleagues seemed especially committed to advancing the careers of high-performing Black professionals. Sandra posited that although Black associates at times had to overcome negative racial biases to establish themselves in the eyes of their colleagues, those who were able to do so often found enthusiastic allies and supporters. She noted, "I really do think that we have to work harder. But I think that if you do work harder and people notice you, and some of this is probably to assuage White guilt, but I think there's been some people to take a real interest in me like, 'I can help this Black kid make it.'" Diana, an associate who later made nonequity partner at her law firm, offered a similar perspective based on her own experiences. Diana reported that being Black had helped her attract attention from partners who were impressed by her work performance and eventually became useful mentors and sponsors.

Sandra was also mindful of the risks of mistreatment on the basis of race. She contrasted her positive relationships with more discomforting interactions she had with other senior White colleagues. She recalled one such incident in which a White partner mistook her for a member of their firm's support staff: "A couple years ago there was an older partner in the hallway, and I was standing by my printer. It was after hours, and he was like, 'Hey, are you the one I was working with earlier?' And I was just like 'what?' And he said, 'I can't get my computer to work.' Then I realized that he thought I was a secretary, so I just looked at him like he was crazy and walked back into my office."

Although this incident hardly affected Sandra, many Black professionals might have found it deeply offensive or even demoralizing. But because she already enjoyed good relationships with other White partners, instead of making her anxious about how White partners perceived her, the microaggression just bounced off her. "I thought 'wow, that was crazy!'" she said. "I just had to shake that off."

This was not the only such experience that Sandra encountered. She also recalled an instance in which a different partner's overblown reaction to her stellar performance on an assignment led her to suspect that he had expected less of her because of her race.

> I was working on a pro bono case, and it was an appellate brief that I was working on, so [the partner] wasn't that involved. He was like, "it's due next week, just give me a draft a couple days before—I'll edit it." And so I sent him the draft when I was done. And he comes down to my office, and he has this sort of look on his face, this sort of stunned look, and I was like "Is everything ok?" and he was like, "You *write so well.*" . . . And I was like, "I'm sorry, why are you shocked that I can conjugate verbs? You shouldn't be. I'm a lawyer, and I work here." . . . [T]he way it came off to me was like, "Oh my god, I can't believe it!"

Although intended as a compliment, the partner's surprised reaction signaled that he possibly held Black associates in low regard. But because of her prior experiences and her superlative abilities, these interactions barely affected Sandra. Instead, Sandra's racial habitus and successes at the firm led her to perceive racial disadvantages as temporary challenges that talented Black professionals could overcome through strategic effort: "All I'm saying is that there is a certain savviness that I think you can adopt to make things better and to combat some of the probably inherent racist notions that a lot people probably have. . . . I'm saying that they're definitely there but I don't know that they're necessarily deal breakers. At least that has not been my experience—not yet. I'll keep you posted."

Conclusion

There are any number of reasons that some Black professionals fare better than others at elite firms. Differences in talent, luck, and determination all likely play important roles in contributing to intraracial variations in career outcomes. White familiarity, the sense of ease that some Black professionals have based on their prior social interactions and relationships with other White people in other White spaces, also helps Black professionals thrive by protecting them against racial discomfort. The relative comfort of Black professionals with prior interracial acclimation is the counterpoint to the problems of racial discomfort detailed in the preceding chapters. Although White familiarity does not guarantee that Black professionals will have successful or satisfying careers at these firms, it can increase their chances.

CONCLUSION

A New Understanding of Inequality at Elite Firms

In this book I have offered new insights into the long-standing problem of racial inequality at elite professional services firms. The failure of these firms to achieve fairer and more inclusive work environments, and the resulting disadvantages inflicted upon Black professionals, have already been documented and examined at length in other works. Countless books, articles, and essays have weighed in on these problems, and firms have expended considerable resources in their efforts to ameliorate them. But the lived experiences of the Black professionals whom I interviewed for this book reveal that there is still much to be learned about the challenges that Black professionals face. Their accounts of their careers and their broader life experiences shed new light on certain subtle social dynamics that had been overlooked in previous writings. The racial difficulties that they described often involved nuanced challenges arising from the structural and social conditions that shaped careers within these firms. Specifically, many reported experiencing intense racial discomfort about being constantly forced to navigate unfamiliar White-dominated social settings and precarious work situations in which they perceived themselves to be at risk of discrimination. This racial discomfort consisted of two separate components, social alienation and stigma anxiety, that both disadvantage Black professionals by impeding their access to beneficial workplace relationships, premium work assignments, and professional esteem and accolades.

Social alienation, the isolation and frustration that many Black professionals experience because their backgrounds and preferences differ from those of their White colleagues, is part of a process that marginalizes them within these firms. Stigma anxiety, the uneasiness and trepidation that Black professionals experience when they expect to be treated unfairly, also contributes to inequitable employment outcomes. These forms of racial discomfort are especially harmful for Black professionals at elite firms, where professionals' relationships and rapport with colleagues are immensely important because their careers are determined by the discretionary actions and subjective assessments of their predominantly White senior colleagues. Depriving Black professionals of access to career capital and subjecting them to stress and frustration, racial discomfort ultimately leads them to leave their firms at higher rates and on worse terms than their White counterparts. This limits the careers of Black professionals even if they personally never suffer any acts of racial bias.

Racial discomfort is a complex problem and arises from causes both within and outside of these firms. It is the product of broad societal discrimination and segregation, and of racial disparities and institutional discrimination common at elite firms. The specific actions and decisions of White professionals that exacerbate racial discomfort—such as their choice of conversational topics and venues for social gatherings—often seem innocuous. But cumulatively, even seemingly trivial matters can further marginalize Black professionals as outsiders. Worse, racial discomfort is difficult to recognize and easy to misinterpret. When Black professionals disengage from workplace interactions and office life because of racial discomfort, their colleagues may see them as unfriendly, lacking self-confidence, or uninterested in their careers at their firms. The successes of other Black professionals may fuel these misperceptions by suggesting that these firms are racially fair and that Black professionals who struggle therefore have only themselves to blame. But my research offers another explanation for these intraracial differences: White familiarity from prior relationships with White family and friends gives its beneficiaries greater ease in White spaces. This insulates them against racial discomfort, advantaging them substantially over other Black professionals.

My findings concerning racial discomfort have implications for academics, elite firms, Black professionals, and workers in other fields. In this chapter I address these in turn.

Scholarly Contributions and Implications

ELITE FIRMS AS WHITE SPACES

The problems of racial discomfort that I discuss throughout this book arise from the Whiteness of elite professional services firms. In illuminating ways that these seemingly raceless or race-neutral firms are actually distinctively White institutions, this book advances existing scholarship on White spaces and racialized institutions.[1] Demographically, symbolically, and culturally, elite professional services firms are White-dominated organizations. These racial attributes may be taken for granted by White professionals and other observers, but they are highly conspicuous to many Black professionals, who often find themselves the only Black people present in White-dominated firm spaces. The taken-for-granted Whiteness of these institutions shapes both everyday interactions and social gatherings, which generally reflect the cultural preferences of firms' White professional majorities. And because of the racial skew of power and representation, to thrive in these firms Black professionals must impress and forge relationships with colleagues who are overwhelmingly White. In these ways, the Whiteness of these firms is central to the challenges that Black professionals encounter within them, including racial discomfort.

CULTURAL DISADVANTAGE

While discussions of White employers' inclusion issues often focus on discrimination and microaggressions, in this book I take a very different approach. This book instead emphasizes the role of culture in contributing to racial inequality in employment, by introducing the concept of social alienation. Just as existing research has already demonstrated that class and gender differences in workers' cultural capital can shape their careers,[2] my findings reveal that race-based differences—though far less frequently discussed in research on employment—may be just as impactful. In the context of White firms, even seemingly trivial racial differences in preferred leisure activities and pop culture can further marginalize Black professionals as social outsiders. This book's discussion of social alienation also uncovers a new form of intersectional cultural disadvantage. Black women and Black professionals from disadvantaged backgrounds often face especially acute social alienation because their gender and class traits further differentiate their cultural capital from that which is valued at their firms. As the accounts of the attorneys Aja and Brandon revealed in chapter 3, these other identity traits can make it even more difficult for Black professionals to build relationships and rapport with peers, influential senior colleagues, and clients. Altogether, these findings suggest that future efforts to understand the difficulties and disadvantages that Black workers experience in White workplaces should devote far greater attention to the contributing role of culture.

NAVIGATING RACIAL RISKS

In developing the concept of stigma anxiety, I build upon insights from several social science disciplines by connecting the internal mental processes that psychologists study with the broad social processes that sociologists and organizational scholars research. My discussion of stigma anxiety explains how the very *risk* of discrimination prevalent in these firms can undermine the careers of Black professionals regardless of whether they actually encounter discrimination. My findings are rooted in the insight that Black professionals are not passive victims of discrimination but rather take strategic measures to attempt to limit their exposure in situations where they perceive heightened risk of unfair treatment. Although other writings have discussed approaches that Black professionals (and other workers) take to manage perceived racial risks of discrimination, this book is the first to consider the various ways in which the coping and defensive mechanisms that Black professionals adopt can undermine their careers just as decisively as the discrimination they seek to avoid.

RECONSIDERING THE PRIMACY OF RACIAL BIAS

My findings raise questions about the prevailing assumption that racial bias is the factor primarily responsible for racial disparities at elite firms. They suggest that racial discomfort accounts for at least some of the difficulties and disparities that experts now typically attribute to racial bias. This is not a cause for celebration or complacency. Instead, it reveals that efforts to achieve more equitable and inclusive workplaces will need to address an even broader array of problems than previously appreciated. The processes of racial discomfort can occur even without any intention by White professionals to exclude their non-White colleagues; racial discomfort can function independently of unconscious bias, too. So even if a firm could eliminate racial bias, Black professionals likely would still experience social alienation and stigma anxiety. White professionals' cultural preferences would still dictate workplace interactions at these firms, and Black professionals would still feel at risk of discrimination, as they would have no way of knowing that their White colleagues were unbiased.

WHITE FAMILIARITY AND THE IMPORTANCE OF EARLIER LIFE EXPERIENCES

Most writings on the difficulties of Black professionals focus specifically on the obstacles and disadvantages they encounter on the job during their careers at their places of employment. In this book I attempt to avoid the limitations of this approach by also considering the potential impact of Black professionals' prior life experiences on their career outcomes. Drawing insights made available through my life-history-style interviews, I find that the segregation that shapes Black and White Americans' lives in childhood and as university students is a key determinant of the racial discomfort Black professionals experience at White firms. Differences in Black professionals' personal backgrounds also help explain some of the profound divergences in their experiences at these firms. By also examining the success stories of those Black professionals most content with their career experiences, this book extends the cultural sociological research on habitus to the study of race and employment.

Addressing Racial Discomfort: What Can Firms Do?

Firms cannot fully eliminate racial discomfort by themselves. So long as racial segregation and discrimination remain prevalent in America, Black people likely will continue to experience racial discomfort in elite firms and other White institutions. And no matter how many resources firm leaders devote to their DEI objectives, these firms may very well remain White spaces in perpetuity. Eradicating racial discomfort would require addressing its root structural causes in societal segregation and inequality, which would entail massive public investments and policy changes of a magnitude that far exceeds the current political will. As a practical matter then, racial discomfort is likely here to stay.

Although firms cannot prevent racial discomfort altogether, they can limit its impact. They can do so through a combination of policies that both provide more equitable treatment to all junior professionals and channel career capital opportunities to Black professionals in need of them. Specifically, firms may be able to make progress by implementing the following five types of measures: (1) career capital monitoring, (2) enhanced mentorship programs and assignment procedures, (3) racial discomfort training, (4) accountability measures and incentives, and (5) discomfort-conscious programming.

MONITORING CAREER CAPITAL DEFICITS

As an initial matter, firms need to collect more comprehensive data regarding individual professionals' access to career capital. Timely, detailed information about emerging deficits and racial disparities in premium assignments and mentorship, for example, can help firms steer resources and opportunities to individual Black professionals who are at risk of negative career outcomes. Firm leaders could also attempt to track individual senior professionals' assignment, mentorship, and sponsorship actions to determine whether they are providing sufficient career capital opportunities to all of their Black junior colleagues.

Firm leaders could supplement this information by seeking regular input from Black professionals about their experiences at the firm. By allowing their diversity personnel or outside experts to convene confidential focus groups or to conduct confidential one-on-one interviews with Black professional employees, firms would be able to give their senior professionals timely information about problems and concerns that they might otherwise fail to detect.

ENHANCED RELATIONSHIP PROGRAMS AND ASSIGNMENT PROCEDURES

Collecting these data could help firms provide additional mentors and sponsors to junior professionals as needed to address any racial deficits in social capital. Such efforts would help junior professionals of all races but would likely benefit Black professionals disproportionately, given the racial disparities in social capital prevalent at these firms. Firms also can adopt targeted mentorship and sponsorship programs that specifically pair Black professionals with particularly supportive and powerful senior colleagues. Formal relationship programs are no substitute for the mentorship and sponsorship relationships that some colleagues form with each other more organically, but research suggests that they can help improve Black workers' career outcomes.[3] Further, firms may be able to make these programs more effective by setting high expectations for the frequency of meetings and mentors' involvement in their mentees' careers and by tracking these relationships to ensure that such expectations are met. In some instances, firms could take advantage of cultural homophily to further strengthen these programs by identifying common interests and other shared traits that might help predominantly White mentors and Black mentees develop rapport.

Firms can use similar measures to address racial disparities in human capital. Firms might address racial disparities in assignments in part through policies that give all junior professionals more equitable access to developmental opportunities, including by further limiting senior professionals' discretion to allocate assignments to their preferred junior colleagues. Firms could also explore alternative staffing arrangements, such as those that assign junior professionals to work exclusively with specific senior colleagues (as somewhat of an apprentice system). Apprentice-style approaches also limit senior professionals' discretion to divvy out work to their preferred junior colleagues by instead requiring them to share their work with the junior colleagues designated to work with them. Such programs do not wholly eliminate the potential for bias and favoritism in staffing, but they could help Black professionals by ensuring that they are working with senior colleagues who have a vested interest in their professional development. Firms especially committed to addressing racial disparities in human capital also could develop racially targeted staffing procedures that allocate opportunities to Black professionals and other employees from marginalized groups in particular. All of these approaches have their limits; they are sure to encounter resistance from at least some senior professionals, and depending on their design, racially targeted staffing procedures may be in tension with employment discrimination law. But in light of the apparent consistency with which Black professionals lack equitable opportunities to develop human capital and the failure of existing policies to resolve this problem, such bold measures may be necessary to make further headway.

TRAINING ON RACIAL DISCOMFORT

One reason racial discomfort is as damaging as it is for Black professionals is that it often either goes unrecognized or is misinterpreted as a personal deficiency. Firms can address this problem by spreading awareness about racial discomfort through training and other communication initiatives.

Most firms already provide extensive training on DEI topics, but this existing training suffers from several shortcomings. Current training programs that disproportionately focus on implicit bias may in some instances be counterproductive, as White employees required to attend such sessions can become resentful and defensive.[4] Additionally, by raising awareness of the prevalence of bias, this training may inadvertently help normalize it, potentially making trainees *more* likely to discriminate.[5] Further, implicit bias training actually may exacerbate racial discomfort by increasing Black professionals' anxiety about latent threats of discrimination at their firms. For these reasons, the current bias-oriented training approaches do not appear to significantly reduce racial bias or improve outcomes for Black employees.[6]

Firms might enhance their training offerings by expanding them to cover social alienation and stigma anxiety. This training could help reduce the impact of racial discomfort in a number of ways. First, it would increase cultural competency among professionals by teaching them about how taken-for-granted cultural preferences that privilege many White professionals and marginalize many Black professionals commonly shape workplace interactions and office outings. By helping senior professionals better understand racial discomfort, this training could help them avoid misinterpreting Black professionals' discomfort-driven behavior as indicating that they are uninterested, unconfident, or unfriendly, when assessing their performance. This training may also benefit Black professionals by providing them more insights into their difficulties at these firms, and they may appreciate knowing that thanks to this training, their non-Black colleagues also better understand their experiences. This training can also equip Black professionals with information useful for navigating their careers in these firms. It can help ensure that all professionals appreciate the critical importance of developing social capital with White colleagues. Finally, it is worth noting that training on racial discomfort may also be less susceptible to the White resistance that undermines bias training; White workers who dismiss or react defensively to information about implicit bias may be more receptive to learning about homophily, stigma consciousness, and racial anxiety.

INCENTIVES AND ACCOUNTABILITY

Firms can also reduce the impact of racial discomfort by further incentivizing senior professionals to support their Black colleagues. Some firms have begun taking steps in this direction.[7] The law firm Paul Weiss is one example. After a 2018 announcement including pictures of the twelve attorneys in its newly elected partnership class went viral because all of the new partners were White, Paul Weiss implemented a set of reforms that included tying partners' compensation to their performance related to diversity and inclusion.[8] Dozens of the nation's largest law firms joined the "Do Something Hard" initiative, in accordance with which they vow to take into account individual partners' staffing and retention of non-White attorneys when determining their bonuses.[9] Such compensation-based measures may help induce senior professionals to allocate career capital more equitably.

Firms can also leverage nonfinancial incentives. Researchers have identified a social accountability effect that occurs when supervisors who know that their performance data will be shared with colleagues strive to achieve better outcomes in order to improve their reputation among their peers.[10] Putting partners and department leaders on notice that statistics of each departments' diversity outcomes will be shared throughout the firm and discussed at firm leadership meetings could trigger this effect. Making diversity performance data available to professionals and potential job seekers may provide even greater accountability while also helping Black professionals make more informed decisions about where to pursue their careers and may help diversity-minded clients decide which firms to hire. Accordingly, this transparency would give firms strong incentives to allocate work opportunities more equitably. Finally, firms also could request that partners and department leaders track and report their informal social contacts with colleagues, including lunches, dinners, and impromptu mentorship sessions.

DISCOMFORT-CONSCIOUS PROGRAMMING

Given the racial demographics of elite firms—particularly in their senior ranks—and their clients, it may be inevitable that informal social events, networking events, and other firm activities will largely reflect White tastes and preferences, exposing Black professionals to the risk of social alienation. Nevertheless, firms can take steps to make at least some firm-related events less uncomfortable for Black professionals (and other professionals who are not straight White men). Firms should make sure that the groups of professionals who plan firm-sponsored events are diverse to better ensure that these events take into consideration the various tastes of the firm's professional workforce. Firms can also encourage senior professionals to mind the possible inadvertent exclusionary impact of some of their informal outings and to consider designing events that might appeal to a broader cross-section of firm employees. Firm leaders and the leaders of firms' Black professional affinity groups can also work together to encourage White senior professionals to attend more affinity group functions, to make themselves available to network with more junior Black professionals in more comfortable spaces where the Black professionals may be less likely to experience social alienation or

stigma anxiety. These suggestions offer at best only hope for marginal progress, but even modest DEI gains can be highly valuable,
given the vexing nature of racial discomfort.

Not all approaches toward addressing the effects of racial discomfort are equally valid. There are also means of addressing
racial discomfort that firms should refrain from using to avoid
becoming even more racially exclusionary. For example, firms not
fully committed to becoming equitable and inclusive work settings
might consider subjecting Black candidates to additional scrutiny
to screen out those who seem most at risk of discomfort. Or they
might redirect their recruiting practices away from HBCUs, where
investment banks and management consulting firms now recruit
significant numbers of their incoming Black professionals. Such
measures may seem tempting, but they would essentially raise
discriminatory barriers for qualified Black candidates. Instead of
making it harder for aspiring Black professionals to get their feet
in the door, firms should focus on making their workplaces more
equitable and inclusive.

A ROLE FOR INDIVIDUAL WHITE PROFESSIONALS

There are limits to what the policies described here can accom-
plish. Further progress will require additional voluntary efforts
from individual White professionals interested in helping their
firms become more equitable and inclusive. As members of the
dominant in-group, White professionals have the power to enhance the careers of their Black colleagues by taking steps to
lessen the impact of racial discomfort. They can help reduce social alienation by using more inclusive interactional habits, for
example by engaging in more open-ended discussions that draw
out the interests and experiences of colleagues instead of centering conversations around their own interests.[11] White senior pro-

fessionals can use their discretion to go above and beyond any firm-level policies by purposefully providing Black professionals with opportunities, mentorship, and sponsorship, and by giving them the benefit of the doubt when assessing their work performance. White senior professionals can help reduce the impact of racial reticence by initiating more frequent interactions and in-depth conversations with their Black colleagues and by soliciting their input during team meetings and in other workplace interactions. Finally, although White professionals could in theory work to become more culturally proficient by intentionally acclimating themselves to the cultural capital more popular among their Black colleagues, such efforts are fraught with risk. Attempting to use Black cultural capital to establish rapport with Black colleagues could easily come across as awkward, unnatural, or even offensive—potentially making their Black colleagues even more anxious about racial stigma.

What Can Black People Do?

In ideal circumstances, racial discomfort would be irrelevant to Black professionals' careers. They would thrive (or fail) at these firms purely according to the quality of their performance, reflecting their talent and effort. Their prior interracial social relationships and interactions would be immaterial to their professional fate. But in the real world, succeeding at elite firms requires more than technical competence and hard work. Social capital plays an outsized role in shaping professionals' careers; those who are most adept at developing relationships and rapport with colleagues will tend to fare better than their counterparts. Because of racial discomfort, this social dimension of professional careers is especially challenging for many Black professionals.

STRATEGIC ACCLIMATION AND ACCULTURATION

Fortunately, Black professionals are not completely powerless in the face of these challenges. Through strategic effort, some may be able to mitigate the impact of racial discomfort on their careers. For example, they may lessen their risk of social alienation by working to familiarize themselves with the cultural capital that holds currency in their offices. Michael, the former investment banker, endorsed this approach. He recommended that to better develop relationships with senior White sponsors and mentors, Black junior professionals should "figure out what people like to do outside of the office when they're not at work, and then go develop those mutual things outside of the office that might help you in the office." Other interviewees described using similar tactics. Lerone, who had struggled with social alienation early in his career, managed to develop more common ground with his White colleagues by making it a point to partake in and consume certain cultural experiences and items that were popular among them. He described purposefully vacationing at locales that he had heard them discuss, and he purchased luxury items including fine wines and expensive watches to better fit in with them. Lerone credits these efforts with helping him become more of an insider, helping him overcome the cultural disadvantages that had hindered him earlier in his career.

As a strategy for Black advancement, strategic acculturation has important downsides. It can spare Black professionals (and aspiring Black professionals) from some of the hardships of racial discomfort, but it is not without costs. Strategic acculturation arguably unfairly burdens Black people by requiring them to immerse themselves in unfamiliar and potentially unwelcoming social settings, while their White counterparts remain free to pursue their preferred interests and proclivities. Developing this interracial acclimation can require Black professionals to expend considerable time, energy, and financial resources—and for uncertain returns. This disproportionate burden is unfair, and it can be frustrating and stressful even for those Black professionals who ultimately benefit from this approach. A related concern is that instead of challenging the Whiteness of elite firms, strategic acculturation further legitimizes it by accepting that Black professionals should work to attain White cultural traits. Treating strategic acculturation as a reasonable obligation that Black professionals should take on in order to pursue careers in these firms could lead people to treat social alienation as a failure on the part of the individual Black professionals who are unable to acclimate themselves.

Although these concerns are understandable, many Black professionals may find that the benefits of strategic acculturation outweigh its costs. Working at elite firms already requires them to bear the extra burden of accommodating their White colleagues' often unfamiliar tastes and interests, which many of them find challenging. Responsibility for interracial acclimation should not fall on Black professionals alone. But as White professionals constitute the majority of the workforces at these firms, they have far less incentive to acclimate themselves to the cultural traits of other groups. Whether or not Black professionals equip themselves to navigate the cultural milieu of these firms, workplace interactions likely will continue to disproportionately reflect the experiences and preferences of White professionals for the foreseeable future. By reducing Black professionals' vulnerability to social alienation, strategic acculturation may increase their prospects for succeeding at elite firms, potentially putting them in a position to one day help diversify their firms' cultural milieu as influential senior professionals.

HELPING FUTURE GENERATIONS OF BLACK PROFESSIONALS

For those who are not isolated by racial segregation, it can be much easier to develop interracial acclimation earlier in life. The White familiarity that boosts the careers of some Black professionals reflects years—often decades—of prior experience. Although residential and school segregation continues to limit the interactions of most Black and White children, and the United States Supreme Court has limited the ability of school districts to achieve greater school integration,[12] millions of Black children do attend predominantly White elementary and secondary schools, and thousands of Black students attend selective predominantly White colleges and professional schools. These facts present a potential for far more extensive interracial interaction than presently occurs. Greater integration in student life might provide many Black students with protection against racial discomfort later in life, when they enter the workforce and assume positions at White institutions.

Based on this logic, some of my respondents used their class resources to immerse their children in racially integrated living and learning environments, to ensure that they would be comfortable in non-Black settings as adults. Rachel, the attorney, discussed working to give her young son social experiences and cultural capital that she believed would help him navigate non-Black environments later in life: "My son is going to be well-traveled. He will likely have been to Europe before he gets to junior high. He's gonna know two-and-a-half languages. . . . By the time he gets to college, he won't be in any unfamiliar place. I think the more we expose our young people to these environments earlier, [the better]."

In seeking to prepare her son culturally and socially to thrive in varied institutional and social spaces, Rachel's approach ultimately might improve his prospects at predominantly White firms. Similarly, people and organizations who mentor aspiring Black professionals may boost their career prospects at elite, predominantly White firms by encouraging or providing access to instrumentally beneficial acculturation.

A ROLE FOR UNIVERSITIES?

College and professional school may present the best opportunities for interracial immersion. The highly selective universities from which elite professional services firms hire most of their junior-level talent are more diverse than most elementary and secondary schools, and students at these universities live in closer proximity to members of other racial groups than at any other time in their lives. For those who are interested, this proximity presents potential opportunities for developing White familiarity. And as young adults are still forming their social identities and acquiring their cultural sensibilities in college, this may be an opportune time to seek exposure to the cultural traits of others.[13] To be sure, Black students may find pursuing such acclimation in college difficult. College life is rife with racialized social patterns, microaggressions, and egregious racial incidents.[14] These conditions can make seeking out interracial acclimation uncomfortable and potentially risky. Nonetheless, these years likely provide the most viable opportunities for interracial social exposure for many future Black (and White) professionals.

Meaningful increases in interracial friendships and social acclimation on campus likely will only occur if universities take a more active role in facilitating interracial interactions.[15] Most importantly, universities must work to establish a campus climate more conducive to interracial interactions and to ensure that Black students find their campuses welcoming. This is a tall order, but they can make headway by implementing policies that ensure the prompt resolution of Black students' racial concerns.[16] Hiring more diverse faculty, administrators, and university leaders may also help make campuses feel more inclusive for Black students.[17] Universities can further facilitate interracial interactions through various educational policies, including diversity-oriented curricular measures, extracurricular programming, and targeted roommate assignment practices.[18] Universities should also reevaluate some of their programming that tends to exacerbate racial separateness. Although some of these programs and resources— including racially separate admitted students' events and racially themed housing—can help some Black students immensely by providing them with support and a sense of belonging on campuses they might otherwise find isolating or racially threatening,[19] schools interested in reducing racial discomfort should be mindful of the drawbacks of such arrangements and think about ways to supplement or amend them.

BLACK-OWNED FIRMS AS AN ALTERNATIVE?

It is also worth noting that although some Black professionals, like Nakia in chapter 2, avoid racial discomfort by pursuing racial employment in Black-owned firms, this is simply not a viable or desirable solution for many of the Black professionals who pursue careers at elite White firms. Although Black-owned firms exist in law, investment banking, and consulting, they are far fewer in number and smaller in size than large White firms. Some of the largest Black-owned law firms in America have fewer total Black attorneys than the largest White firms have in their first-year classes alone. The largest minority-owned investment banks have hundreds of employees in total, while the largest investment banks have thousands of investment bankers alone.[20] These Black-owned firms simply cannot accommodate the thousands of Black professionals who join large White firms each year. Just as importantly, elite firms give junior professionals unparalleled access to wealth, social capital, and prestige that these smaller firms are not able to replicate. They cannot offer comparable financial compensation or position their professionals for the types of subsequent employment opportunities that the most prestigious White firms do.

Discomfort Beyond the Black Elite

The Black professionals whose experiences are examined in this book are a select group, and they account for only a very small percentage of the American workforce. The elite firms where they have worked are a rarified domain very different from the occupational contexts of most other US employees.

Yet their experiences with racial discomfort at these firms are not entirely unique. Many different types of workers in a variety of settings may encounter similar problems. Racial discomfort also affects Black workers in other occupations that share the same characteristics as professional positions at elite firms. So long as they work at White institutions where employers and supervisors exercise discretion and subjective judgment in allocating career capital and opportunities for advancement, other Black workers will face similar challenges.

Although Black workers may be especially susceptible to racial discomfort because of the heightened stigma and segregation that Black Americans experience, workers from other marginalized groups may experience analogous disadvantages. Prior research has demonstrated that White women and upwardly mobile White workers from lower social class backgrounds also experience social alienation and stigma anxiety in work settings that are dominated by men or by people from more affluent backgrounds.[21] Workers from other racial groups can also experience racial discomfort, though the impact of social alienation and stigma anxiety on them should vary according to the content of their groups' stereotypes and the extent of their social distance from White Americans. For example, Latinx workers, who are stereotyped as incompetent, and Asian workers, who are stereotyped as cold and unfriendly, may experience stigma anxiety in different situations that lead them to employ different defensive and coping mechanisms. Professionals from other marginalized groups, including religious minorities and LGBTQ+ people, may experience both stigma anxiety and social alienation to the extent that their identities are subject to stigma and their cultural capital and social preferences differ from those predominant at their firms.

This book is the culmination of many years that I have spent studying, writing, and speaking about the potential disadvantages that Black professionals encounter at elite firms. In it, I have attempted to move beyond the conventional focus on racial bias to call attention to other major impediments that for too long have been overlooked and misunderstood. I hope that scholars, firms, Black professionals, and other workers will find this book a helpful resource for thinking about, navigating, and addressing the problems of racial discomfort. There are no easy solutions to these challenges. The most viable reforms will require sustained effort and commitment on the part of many different people and institutions. And the hard-fought gains it makes possible will almost certainly occur slowly and incrementally. But these efforts are worth pursuing nevertheless. The future progress of Black professionals at elite firms and other predominantly White workplaces may depend on doing so.

Acknowledgments

This book has been a long journey, and I owe thanks to many people and institutions.

First and foremost, I owe immense gratitude to the many people who allowed me to interview them for this project. These interviewees were extraordinarily generous in their willingness to share with me not only their time but also their candid reflections about sensitive topics. To the extent that this book has anything interesting to say about race in the workplace, it is in large part thanks to them. I am also indebted to the people who graciously extended themselves to make their social and professional networks available to me by spreading word of my research, vouching for me, and encouraging their contacts to participate in this study.

I began working on the research that developed into this book at Princeton University while enrolled in the sociology and social policy joint degree program. My classmates and cohort members in the Sociology Department and in the joint degree program offered valuable insights and camaraderie throughout my time there. I also benefited immensely from the support of my mentor and graduate school adviser, Katherine Newman, who urged me to expand this study because she sensed that I had something interesting to say about the nuances of race in elite work settings.

Kathy guided me through all of the early stages of this project, including the development of my interview questions, planning the collection of my sample, and the initial analysis of my qualitative data. This project has evolved quite a bit since those early days, but her attention and guidance helped me build a great foundation. I also benefited from advice from Devah Pager, who as a member of my dissertation committee pushed me to think about my research more expansively and to be bold enough to develop original ideas about the significance of race for Black professionals. ("What is 'the Kevin Woodson theory' of race at these firms?" she once asked me.)

Over the course of my career as a law professor I have been blessed with generous and engaged colleagues and deans, first at the Thomas R. Kline School of Law at Drexel University and now at the University of Richmond School of Law. My deans, first Roger Dennis and Dan Filler at Drexel and then Wendy Purdue at the University of Richmond, were each highly encouraging, supportive, and patient while I spent years sharpening my ideas and reframing and revising the material that eventually became this book. A number of my colleagues at these schools have listened to me discuss my research at length and have provided insightful feedback at different stages of the writing process. My writing buddy, Corinna Lain, was especially helpful in providing accountability and encouragement as I completed my manuscript.

I have also benefited immensely from feedback I received at a number of conferences and workshops over the years. In addition to fellowship and friendship, my "Langston brothers," the participants in the various John Mercer Langston annual writing workshops, gave me valuable feedback that informed how I thought and wrote about my research. There are too many names to attempt to thank them individually, but I appreciate the support and feedback of Chris Tyson, Gregory Parks, Jonathan Glater, Terry Smith, Etienne Toussaint, Kenya Smith, Frank Rudy Cooper, Vinay

Harpalani, Cedric Powell, Goldburn Maynard, Mitch Crusto, and many others. I am especially grateful to Charlton Copeland and Matthew Shaw for their detailed comments on my prospectus materials and for extensive phone conversations on this project. At a session at a Northeast People of Color Legal Scholarship Conference, Solangel Maldonado helped me greatly by pushing me to reframe how I positioned my contributions in relation to the discourse on racial bias. Participants of a symposium at Fordham University School of Law, The Challenge of Equity and Inclusion in the Legal Profession: An International and Comparative Perspective, also improved my research with their thoughtful questions and comments. At these and other conferences I benefited from kind and constructive words from law professors Stacey Hawkins, Mario Barnes, Terry Smith, and Devon Carbado, among others. The faculties of the University of Pittsburgh School of Law, the University of Miami School of Law, and the Wake Forest University School of Law each also offered illuminating comments and suggestions during my faculty workshop presentations at their institutions. This book also benefited from comments, questions, and feedback from attorneys who sat through presentations and discussions of my research at various ABA and state and local bar conferences and workshops, as well as at a Black History Month event at my former law firm, WilmerHale, in 2022.

I am also grateful to Elizabeth Branch Dyson at the University of Chicago Press for helping me make this book what it is. As a first-time book author, I especially appreciated her guidance through the post-submission and revision phases, which helped make the publication process as smooth as possible. I also thank her for helping me make the book more readable and accessible to broader audiences.

I owe gratitude to many friends and loved ones for their support and encouragement over the years. Bret Asbury, my dear friend and former colleague, has read drafts—in some instances multiple versions—of virtually everything I have ever written involving this research, including each of my law review articles and the chapters of this book. His insightful comments were indispensable, and this book is better because of them. Over the years Stephen Bailey has offered useful thoughts about this book and valuable insights into how employers and nonacademics might receive it. Ejike Uzoigwe read drafts of multiple chapters of this book, and his enthusiasm over the years about the book's potential impact encouraged me to push forward. More importantly, since we first met as college freshmen in 1996, more than any other person Ejike has pushed me to challenge conventional wisdom concerning race in America, to clarify my own thoughts about the topic, and to boldly develop and share my ideas. This book may never have been written had Tiffanie Woodards not encouraged me to return to graduate school in a conversation circa 2005. Tiffanie has been supportive of me and enthusiastic about this book project ever since. This book also benefited immensely from early conversations with the always insightful Bryan Brooks. I am also grateful to Candice Boucaud for her support, patience, and encouragement during an especially frustrating period when I was struggling to make progress on this book. I would also like to thank Tique Oriol, Jeff Potter, Cie-Jai Brown, Elliot Doomes, Amuche Chukudebelu, James Martin, Alex Campbell, Terrance Richardson, and Rahsan Boykin for their friendship and support over the years.

I am especially thankful for Rowena Crabbe's excellent advice, support, encouragement, critiques, and detailed line edits during the final stretch of this book project. In late 2021, when I was still struggling to bring this book to a close, Rowena became an unwavering source of enthusiasm and helped push me to the finish line. To say that the insightful substantive and stylistic comments on each of my draft chapters and the thoughts that she shared during our many conversations about my research greatly improved this book would be a huge understatement. This book would be far, far worse off without her contributions and likely not even finished yet.

I would like to thank my mother, Irene Woodson, for all that she has done for me. Her support for and pride in my academic achievements and professional work have always been one of my main motivations, from childhood to this day. I greatly appreciate the kindness, enthusiasm, and patience she showed me throughout my time working on this book. I would like to thank her, my brother, Keith Woodson, and my father, Kenneth Woodson, for loving me unconditionally. I am also grateful for the love and support of Randy Singer, Laura Jane Woodson, the Woodson family, the Singer family, the Teel family, and the DiMario family.

And to the many other people who have helped me along the way, but whom I somehow have forgotten to mention: I am so sorry! I sincerely hope that you do not interpret my failure to mention you as a lack of gratitude.

APPENDIX A

Data and Methods

This study was inspired by my experience working as an attorney for three years at an elite law firm. As an attorney, I had many conversations with other Black professionals—both colleagues and acquaintances who worked elsewhere—about our experiences at our respective firms. They had a wide variety of experiences at their firms and diverse viewpoints about the impact of race (or lack thereof) on their careers. Unsurprisingly, these discussions often touched upon issues of race. Many of my acquaintances felt disadvantaged by their status as Black professionals, but few spoke of experiencing or observing any blatant discrimination. Others suggested that race did not seem to be a particularly important factor in their careers, but others insisted that Black professionals at their firms—themselves included—were frequently the victims of blatant, thinly veiled racial bias. These conversations made it clear that these firms presented a variety of potential challenges for Black professionals and affected some far more than others, and I sensed that the existing research and reporting did not fully capture the nuances of their experiences. Years later I undertook this study to attempt to shed further light on the complexities of race at elite firms.

Data Collection and Interview Methods

DEVELOPING MY SAMPLE

In undertaking this study I sought to develop a broad, diverse sample that would include Black professionals who had worked in different firms, industries, and cities, including some who no longer worked for elite firms. Snowball sampling, wherein successive contacts and interviewees are asked to recommend this study to other potential interviewees, seemed to be the most feasible method for assembling such a sample.[1] Black professionals potentially face career-threatening consequences for criticizing their employers or even for seeming to be preoccupied with issues of race, so referrals from friends and personal acquaintances may have been especially helpful in making interviewees comfortable participating in this study.[2]

My personal background and demographic characteristics also helped a great deal in developing this sample. Because I am Black (biracial) and previously worked as an attorney at a large law firm, I shared mutual acquaintances with a number of interviewees. Many interviewees were likely more willing to participate in this study and discuss their experiences fully and candidly with a person they believed could relate to aspects of their experiences. My background knowledge about various aspects of corporate workplaces and careers also enhanced our conversations and helped me establish rapport with my interviewees, especially in my interviews with other attorneys.

In gathering the sample I sought out Black people who currently work, or have recently worked, in professional or managerial positions at large, predominantly White firms or corporations. I began by developing a recruitment-solicitation message explaining that I was attempting to study race in America from the perspective of young Black professionals and that I was interested in interviewing Black professionals who were roughly twenty-eight to thirty-three years old and who had experience working in corporate settings. The message explained that the interviews, which would be recorded with their permission, would focus on their childhoods and family backgrounds, educational trajectories, professional experiences, and views about the significance of race in the careers of Black professionals at their firms, including themselves.

I sent copies of this message via email and a social networking website to forty people in my extended social and professional networks, including former college and professional school classmates, professional acquaintances, and current graduate students. For this first group of potential interviewees and referral sources, I made efforts to select a demographically diverse group of people who did not have close ties with one another and who had achieved different levels of success at their firms. I ultimately interviewed approximately half of this group, and several of them referred me to other Black professionals in their networks. In order to increase the reach of the ultimate sample and the diversity of their referrals, I selected people who had attended a variety of different schools and worked for different firms in different geographic areas in varied industries. I invited those contacts that fit the study's criteria to participate in an interview. I asked them and the noneligible contacts to refer me to other eligible young Black professionals. I then asked their referrals to refer me to additional Black professionals, and so on.

In developing these referral chains, I asked that referrers share my message with whatever eligible Black professionals they believed might be willing to participate. To attempt to mitigate the risk of selection bias inherent in snowball sampling, I emphasized that I was interested in speaking with a wide variety of prospective interviewees no matter what their experiences, perspectives, or current professional circumstances were. This approach may have helped me capture a diverse range of professionals, including those who had positive and negative experiences at elite firms and those who no longer worked at these firms. The interviewees generated from these referral chains formed the majority of this study's sample.[3]

Through this sampling method I was able to assemble a diverse, far-reaching sample. The 110 interviewees ranged in age from twenty-six to forty, although the majority were between twenty-eight and thirty-two. They represented a diverse cross-section of undergraduate institutions including Ivy League (29), public (29), private (30), historically Black schools (21), and a military academy (1). Interviewees with professional degrees represented thirty-five professional schools, although a majority (58 of 99) had attended Ivy League or similarly highly ranked schools. The majority (75) were attorneys who had worked as associates at a combined seventy law firm offices. Interviewees had also worked in other industries, including the financial sector (26) and management consulting (12). I also interviewed a number of people who had worked in corporate management and other fields, but I ultimately removed these interviewees from my sample so that I could focus more narrowly on describing the experiences of Black professionals who had worked at professional services firms.

THE INTERVIEWS

At the start of each interview I reiterated the focuses of my study and asked that the interviewee describe their experiences growing up, including their family backgrounds and their experiences in school. I asked clarifying and follow-up questions throughout the interview. I also asked interviewees about the significance of race (or lack thereof) in their childhood experiences, including in their relations with other children and school personnel. I also asked them about their higher education and professional careers, including their perceptions about the impact of race. This approach ensured that the interviews would cover all relevant topics while also allowing interviewees opportunities to share their experiences and perspectives fully and to focus at length on the particular topics they found most pertinent.[4] This open-ended interviewing method helped uncover unexpected insights and allowed for new theories to emerge from the data relatively unconstrained by any preexisting hypotheses.[5]

Most of the interviews in my final sample were conducted by phone, primarily via a conference-call service that allowed me to record and download mp3 files of each interview. Ten interviews were conducted in person. Qualitative research methodologists have discussed at length the possible advantages and drawbacks of conducting interviews by phone instead of in person.[6] For many years the conventional wisdom disfavored phone interviews as inadequate substitutes for in-person interviews that should only be used for limited purposes and if necessary.[7] The perceived drawbacks of conducting interviews by telephone arise from the unavailability of nonverbal communication, which is thought to impede interviewers from developing rapport with respondents and to increase respondents' discomfort, possibly leading to less detailed interviews.[8]

More recently qualitative researchers have come to accept phone interviews as just as legitimate and useful as in-person interviews. A chief advantage of telephone interviews is that they are more convenient and efficient for the interviewer and interviewees alike.[9] This may be especially important for interviewing elite professionals, who have busy and often unpredictable schedules. The flexibility and efficiency of phone interviews were critical, given my objective of gathering a geographically diverse sample. Finally, some interviewees may also be more comfortable discussing sensitive topics by phone.[10] Consistent with the insights of these researchers, I did not detect noticeable differences in the length, level of detail, or substantive views expressed in the interviews conducted in person compared to those conducted by phone.[11]

Interviews ranged in time from approximately thirty minutes to over three hours, with most lasting between sixty and ninety minutes. Upon completing these interviews, I transcribed, summarized, and coded the data for later analysis.

ANALYZING THE DATA

I coded these interviews in a comprehensive spreadsheet capturing interviewees' personal characteristics, attributes of their firms and departments, and views about their professional careers and the significance of race at their firms. Over the course of conducting my interviews, I regularly updated and expanded this coding protocol, including by recoding prior interviews retroactively, ultimately capturing dozens of variables in total.

I did not set out to identify racial disadvantages per se; I was just as interested in understanding the perspectives of Black professionals who did not consider race to be a major source of disadvantage at their firms. But over the years careful analysis of my research and in-depth discussions with scholars and professionals led me to realize the potential value of describing at length the problems of social alienation and stigma anxiety. This book's insights on racial discomfort emerged over years of reviewing and rereading transcripts; reading a variety of social science and legal scholarship; and discussing findings and sharing drafts with other academics, friends, and Black professionals. Research on various types of homophily, a term with which I had not been familiar when I began my research, helped me make sense of the data concerning the role of common ground (and the lack thereof). Years later the bodies of research on stigma consciousness and racial anxiety helped me make sense of and articulate the ongoing concerns and adaptations to perceived threats of workplace bias.

THE DIFFICULTIES OF DETERMINING THE INFLUENCE OF RACE

While conducting my research I have tried to remain mindful of the difficulties inherent in studies such as this that use data based on respondents' reports of their perceptions concerning discrimination and racial fairness. Interviewees' accounts are subject to a number of potential biases and limitations. Determining the role that race has played in any given situation can be extremely difficult. In the context of professional services firms, it requires interpreting the mindsets and motives of other people, including some with whom the interviewee has had minimal contact. This can be a difficult and imprecise process. In order to reach conclusions about the impact of race in their workplaces, people must first think about experiences and disparities they have personally encountered or observed and then consider whether any nonracial explanations, including chance or differences in performance, might account for them. Their perceptions may be distorted by unrepresentative outliers, including particular Black professionals who have been treated especially poorly (or well) and particular White professionals who have been treated especially well (or poorly). And because many elite firms still employ very few Black professionals, individuals may find that there are inadequate "sample sizes" to determine the role of race at their firms.

Perceptions about race are also subject to certain cognitive and social biases. Individual Black professionals have varying levels of stigma consciousness, such that some are far more likely than others to interpret the same fact or incident as evidence of discrimination.[12] Black professionals may also have subconscious psychological motivations that might shape their assessments of their firms' racial climates, potentially leading them to either overstate or downplay the significance of racial disadvantage at their firms.

Psychologists have documented a "self-serving bias" that leads people to attribute unsuccessful outcomes to external factors while taking personal credit for successful ones.[13] In either scenario, this bias could lead Black professionals to emphasize the magnitude of racial disadvantage at their firms, either to avoid blame for their failures or to claim additional credit for their accomplishments in the face of adversity. Attributing their struggles to racism instead of any personal shortcomings may help disappointed Black professionals protect their self-esteem and emotional well-being.[14]

Other factors may lead Black professionals to downplay racial unfairness at their firms. Black professionals who hold ideological beliefs that tend to justify existing racial disparities—for example, faith in meritocracy or belief in racial stereotypes—may be less likely to notice evidence of discrimination.[15] Proponents of systems justification theory posit that people, including the members of disadvantaged groups, are motivated to view society and its institutions as fair, even when this belief runs counter to their own interests.[16] These researchers have theorized that discounting evidence of unfairness therefore may improve the emotional well-being of marginalized individuals by sparing them from psychological distress.[17] Because of these tendencies, some Black professionals may be predisposed to perceive their workplaces as racially fair institutions, even in the face of evidence to the contrary. But notwithstanding these difficulties and potential biases, Black professionals' perspectives about the significance of race at their firms are important to understand and offer potentially valuable insights into the nature of employment inequality.

APPENDIX B

List of Respondents

Pseudonym	Firm Type	Gender
Joshua	Investment banking	Male
Maria	Law	Female
James	Law	Male
Hal	Law	Male
Gabby	Law	Female
Damon	Consulting; investment banking	Male
Jonah	Law	Male
Temi	Law	Female
Ray	Law	Male
Leonard	Law	Male
Henry	Law	Male
Forrest	Investment banking	Male
Heidi	Consulting	Female
Chinelo	Law	Female
Terrance	Law	Male
Indira	Law	Female
Lerone	Investment banking	Male
Kelli	Law	Female
Freda	Investment banking	Female
Scarlett	Investment banking; consulting	Female
Leanne	Law	Female

Pseudonym	Firm Type	Gender
Susan	Law	Female
Brandon	Law	Male
Oscar	Law	Male
Jack	Law	Male
Harold	Law	Male
Brett	Law	Male
William	Investment banking	Male
Cedric	Investment banking	Male
Cornelius	Law	Male
Zeke	Investment banking	Male
Deborah	Law	Female
Prisca	Law	Female
Gloria	Law	Female
Humphrey	Law	Male
Kim	Law	Female
Danielle	Law	Female
Dan	Investment banking	Male
Bobby	Law	Male
Dorothy	Law	Female
Ugo	Investment banking	Male
Agnes	Law	Female
Nathan	Law; investment banking	Male
Pierce	Law	Male
Kenneth	Investment banking	Male
Earl	Law	Male
Aja	Law	Female
LaTonya	Law	Female
Steven	Law	Male
Rachel	Law	Female
Quincy	Law	Male
Regina	Consulting	Female
Tori	Law	Female
Courtney	Law	Male

Pseudonym	Firm Type	Gender
George	Law	Male
Agnes	Law	Female
Brianne	Law	Female
Clark	Investment banking	Male
Christopher	Law	Male
Cathy	Investment banking; consulting	Female
Stacey	Law	Female
Alan	Law	Male
Nakia	Investment banking	Female
Wesley	Law	Male
Donna	Law	Female
Nkomo	Investment banking	Male
Lionel	Law	Male
Demetria	Consulting	Female
Clara	Law	Female
Eva	Law	Female
Caitlin	Law	Female
Ingrid	Law	Female
Lakesha	Law	Female
Michael	Investment banking	Male
Rahsaan	Consulting	Male
Candice	Law	Female
Kevon	Consulting	Male
Harmony	Law	Female
Hillary	Law	Female
Kia	Law	Female
Samantha	Law	Female
Sylvester	Investment banking	Male
Orin	Investment banking	Male
Leondra	Investment banking	Female
Megan	Law	Female
Jerry	Law	Male
Luke	Law	Male

Pseudonym	Firm Type	Gender
Bert	Law	Male
Derrick	Consulting	Male
Brad	Law	Male
Perry	Law	Male
Maurice	Law	Male
Eunice	Investment banking	Female
Shirley	Law	Female
Sandra	Law	Female
Wayne	Law	Male
Allison	Law	Female
Michelle	Investment banking	Female
Katherine	Law	Female
Olivia	Consulting	Female
Beth	Law	Female
Janet	Law	Female
Ian	Consulting	Male
Natalie	Consulting	Female
Greta	Investment banking	Female
Elizabeth	Law	Female
Roberta	Law	Female
Langston	Law	Male
Pernell	Investment banking	Male
Brielle	Law	Female

Notes

Introduction

1   See Libling 2020.
2   See MCCA 2021.
3   Chambers Associate 2021.
4   Chen 2019.
5   Merle and McGregor 2019.
6   Abelson and Bloomberg 2021. See also Cohan 2018.
7   Morgan Stanley 2021 and JPMorgan Chase & Co. 2021.
8   Black senior professionals are likely even more highly underrepresented in the investment banking divisions of these banks, as Black professionals tend to be concentrated in other departments. Similarly, Black law firm partners may be especially underrepresented in the mergers and acquisitions departments that help Wall Street investment banks execute deals and other business transactions. See Olson 2021.
9   See Root 2014; Melaku 2019; Scheiber and Eligon 2019; Wilkins and Gulati 1996, 1998; Donovan 2006; Abelson et al. 2020; and Zraick 2018.
10 For general definitions of bias, see Dovidio et al. 2010 and Hewstone, Rubin, and Willis 2002. For a small sample of the scholarship and commentary discussing racial bias at professional services firms, see Abelson et al. 2020, Nelson et al. 2019, Zraick 2018, Hauser 2018, Alcorn 2021, McLymore 2020, and American Bar Association 2018.
11 While scholars have previously addressed interactions as pathways for racial and gender bias, this book focuses on interactions as sources of other types of disadvantages. See Green and Kalev 2007 and Sturm 2001.
12 Mark 2003.
13 See Pinel 1999, Stephan 2014, and Mendoza-Denton et al. 2002.

14 Collins, Dumas, and Moyer 2017, Higginbotham and Weber 1999, and Hunt 2007.

15 See Melaku 2019 and Wingfield 2012.

16 For a discussion of some universities' attempts to overstate the extent of inter-racial friendship on campus, including by doctoring pictures of student events, see Prichep 2013. For an in-depth discussion of racial separateness on college campuses, see Woodson 2016b.

17 See Woodson 2016b.

18 See Tatum 2017.

19 See Tatum 2017.

20 See Rothstein 2017.

21 Henkel, Dovidio, and Gaertner 2006.

22 Melaku 2019 and Greene 2008. For further discussion of the racialized charac-ter of many White institutions and spaces that are usually regarded as raceless, see Ray 2019, Evans and Moore 2015, and Moore 2008.

23 DiTomaso 2013.

24 Further information about this sample can be found in the appendixes.

25 See Wingfield 2019 and Melaku 2019.

Chapter One

1 Ho 2009, Wald 2009, and Rivera 2015.

2 A growing body of critical race theory scholarship has identified ways in which a wide variety of institutions, including law schools, university campuses, busi-nesses, airports, parks, retail establishments, and neighborhoods, are racialized White spaces. See Bonilla-Silva and Peoples 2022; Capers 2021; Anderson 2015; Ray 2019; Moore 2008, 2020; Evans and Moore 2015; and Evans 2013. These works have explained that the racial character of these White spaces consistently excludes and disadvantages non-White people, particularly Black Americans. While most of these writings consider the racial demographic composition of these institutions to be central features of their White identity, Capers (2021) has argued that even HBCU law schools should be understood as White institutions, on account of their ideological, symbolic, and architectural Whiteness.

3 Patrice 2020.

4 MCCA 2021, Cohan 2018, Alden 2014, and McElhaney 2020.

5 MCCA 2021.

6 Chambers Associate 2021.

7 Bain & Company 2021.

8 Woodson 2015, 2016a; and Melaku 2019.

9 Piazza 2018.

10 Garth and Sterling 2018.

11 Woodson 2015, 2016a; and Melaku 2019.

12 Anderson 2015 and Pearce 2005.

13 Moore 2020.

14 See Galanter and Henderson 2007.

15 See Major, Lindsey & Africa 2017.

16 Woodson 2016c.

17 Woodson 2015.

18 Cultural capital differs qualitatively from other forms of career capital in that most professionals pursue it far less actively and do not use it to measure their careers.

19 Ho 2009 and Rivera 2015.

20 See Sturm 2001.

21 Woodson 2016c and Tippett 2019.

22 Woodson 2016c.

23 Wilkins and Gulati 1996, 1998.

24 Banks 2004 and NBC News 2014.

25 Wilkins and Gulati 1998.

26 Woodson 2016c.

27 Conversely, premium assignments that enable junior professionals to develop human capital lead to a "Matthew Effect," in which senior professionals become more likely to give them additional high-level opportunities. Rigney 2010.

28 Diaz and Dunican 2011 and Nelson 1988.

29 Diaz and Dunican 2011.

30 Chan and Anteby 2016.

31 Chan and Anteby 2016.

32 Woodson 2016c.

33 Amis, Mair, and Mjunir2020.

34 Three thousand billable hours is an extraordinary mark, even by large law firm standards. It is the equivalent of billing approximately sixty hours per week, a number that does not reflect the additional nonbillable hours that attorneys spend at their jobs. Most attorneys at these firms bill closer to two thousand hours per year.

35 Correll et al. 2020.

36 Cappeli and Tavis 2016 and McGregor 2013.

37 Wilkins and Gulati 1996, 1998.

38 The numbers by which performance is measured in these jobs do not always "speak for themselves"; senior professionals can still refer to external factors to rationalize and excuse individual traders' successes and underperformances. Thus, although profit and loss statistics can help Black workers demonstrate their abilities and the value of their contributions, they still do not assure that they will be treated fairly.

39 Castilla 2008 and Correll et al. 2020.

40 Seibert et al. 2001, Hewlett 2013, and Jackson 2016.

41 Rivera 2015, Turner 1960, and Kanter 1977.

42 Murrell, Blake-Beard, and Porter 2021.

43 Methot et al. 2016.

44 Sloan et al. 2013, Anderson 2018, Baldi and McBrier 1997, Payne-Pikus, Hagan, and Nelson 2010, Wilder 2008, James 2000, and Viator 2001.

45 Tilly 1998 and Reeves 2017.

46 This renders racial discomfort difficult to address via employment discrimination law, which usually requires tangible, determinative personnel decisions, including hirings, firings, and demotions. See Woodson 2016a, 2016c.

Chapter Two

1 Coping mechanisms are conscious, voluntary actions in response to external stressors, while defensive mechanisms are subconscious or unconscious reactions (Algorani and Gupta 2021). See also Folkman and Moskowitz 2004.

2 Carbado and Gulati 1999.

3 Goffman 1963, Major and O'Brien 2005, and Crocker et al. 1991.

4 Jones 1987, Hinshaw 2007, Goffman 1963, and Tyler 2020.

5 Inzlicht, Aronson, and Mendoza-Denton 2009.

6 Dovidio et al. 2010, Pinel, Warner, and Chua 2005, and Crocker and Major 1989.

7 Goffman 1963, Loury 2003, Allport 1979 , and Fiske et al. 2002.

8 Taylor et al. 2019.

9 Gaddis 2015, Bertrand and Mullainathan 2004, Pager 2007, Pager and Shephard 2008, and Quillian et al. 2017.

10 Pinel 1999, Link and Phelan 2001, Mendoza-Denton et al. 2002, Page-Gould, Mendoza-Denton, and Mendes 2014, Stephan 2014, Bos et al. 2013, and Lewis et al. 2003.

11 Inzlicht et al. 2006, Inzlicht and Good 2006, Spencer, Logel, and Davies 2016, and Steele and Aronson 1995.

12 Godsil and Richardson 2017.

13 Casad, Petzel, and Ingalls 2019, Lewis and Diamond 2015, and Purdie-Vaughns et al. 2008.

14 Abelson et al. 2020, Nelson et al. 2019, and Dorrian 2022.

15 Melaku 2019.

16 Melaku 2019 and Moore 2020.

17 Social scientists have labeled this phenomenon "tokenism." See Kanter 1977, Wingfield 2010, and Roscigno, Garcia, and Bobbitt-Zeher 2007. The most extreme form of tokenism, which social scientists refer to as "solo status," is thought to make environments especially threatening for members of underrepresented groups. See Niemann and Dovidio 1998, Inzlicht and Good 2006, and Thompson and Sekaquaptewa 2002.

18 Meanwhile, pro-White and pro-Asian stereotypes may lead these professionals to treat underperforming White and Asian professionals more leniently because

they presume them to be intelligent and competent. This "positive" discrimination also produces racial disparities. See Fiske 2012 and Cuddy et al. 2009.

19 Reeves 2014, Dovidio et al. 2010, and Dovidio, Evans, and Tyler 1986.
20 Reeves 2014.
21 Reeves 2014.
22 See Crocker et al. 1991 and Quillian 2006.
23 Pinel 1999, Link and Phelan 2001, Page-Gould, Mendoza-Denton, and Mendes 2014, Stephan 2014, Miller and Kaiser 2001, and Bos et al. 2013.
24 Feagin 1991, Stephan 2014, Mullainathan and Shafir 2013.
25 Pascoe and Richman 2009, Orom et al. 2017, and Travis, Thorpe-Moscon, McCluney 2016.
26 See Dumas, Phillips, and Rothbard 2013 and Phillips, Dumas, and Rothbard 2018.
27 Plant and Devine 2003, Mendoza-Denton et al. 2002, and Pinel 1999.
28 In her book, *You Don't Look Like a Lawyer*, on the experiences of Black female attorneys at New York City law firms, sociologist Tsedale Melaku attests to having experienced these difficulties herself, in a different type of White space. She explained: "Based on my own experience in graduate school, I can certainly affirm the stifling anxieties that attend the prospect of vocalizing questions or comments in such settings: for fear of being wrong—or *worse*—of being judged as incompetent" (Melaku 2019, 52).
29 Thompson and Bolino 2018.
30 See Culver 2018.
31 Ashley 2014.
32 Wingfield 2010 and Evans 2013.
33 Hall et al. 2019 and Williams, Muller, and Kilanski 2012.
34 Devine 1989, Thiem et al. 2019, and Hester and Gray 2018.
35 Carbado and Gulati 2001.
36 Goffman 1963. See Yoshino 2006.
37 McCluney et al. 2019.
38 Collins and Miller 1994 and King 2020.
39 Roberts 2005. See also Dumas, Phillips, and Rothbard 2013.
40 Mark and Harris 2012.
41 Mendoza-Denton and Leiter 2018 and Wang, Stroebe, and Dovidio 2012.
42 Sellers and Shelton 2003.
43 Operario and Fiske 2001, Pinel 2004, Wang, Stroebe, and Dovidio 2012, and Sellers and Shelton 2003.
44 King 2020.

Chapter Three

1 Bourdieu 1986.
2 Lamont and Lareau 1988, Alexander 2004, Rivera 2015, and Mark 2003.

3   Currid-Halkett 2017.

4   Lazarsfeld and Merton 1954, McPherson, Smith-Lovin, and Cook 2001, and Kossinets and Watts 2009.

5   DiMaggio 1987.

6   Although some sociologists use the term *cultural capital* more narrowly, to refer specifically to cultural hierarchies dictated by social elites, this book uses a broader, more flexible understanding of cultural capital as an interactional resource with localized value determined by the cultural preferences of the people present in a given social situation. See Carter 2003.

7   Purcell 2013.

8   Phillips, Dumas, and Rothbard 2018.

9   Rivera 2015.

10   Rivera 2015. See also Neely 2018.

11   Woodson 2015 and King 2020.

12   Kanter 1977 and Rivera 2015. Kanter originally developed this theory to explain why male supervisors consistently favored male workers over their female counterparts in filling high-level positions at a corporation that she studied intensively.

13   Bourdieu 1986, Carter 2003, Patterson 2014, Ridgeway 2019, Purcell 2013, and Erickson 1996.

14   Garth and Sterling 2018.

15   Turco 2010, Purcell 2013, Erickson 1996, and Friedman and Laurison 2019.

16   Patterson 2014.

17   Rivera 2015, Turco 2010, Erickson 1996, Purcell 2013, and Friedman and Laurison 2019.

18   Wilson 1987 and Small, Harding, and Lamont 2010.

19   Claytor 2020, Beasley 2012, and Woodson 2016b.

20   Levin 2017.

21   Levin 2017.

22   Morrissey 2019 and O'Connell 2014.

23   Braxton 1998.

24   *Jet* 1997.

25   May 2014, Mohler 2017, Thompson 2014, and CBS News 2018.

26   Ramsey 2015 and Brock 2012.

27   Rivera 2015.

28   Knox 2019.

29   See Dumas, Phillips, and Rothbard 2013.

30   Dovidio et al. 2010, Hewstone, Rubin, and Willis 2002, Brewer 2001, and Kang 2005.

31   An influential group of antidiscrimination legal scholars has argued that individuals often are subject to racial discrimination according to how they *perform* race, rather than on the basis of their phenotypical characteristics alone. See Carbado and Gulati 1999, 2001, 2013; Yuracko 2006; Rich 2004; Green 2005; and Melaku 2019.

32 Zelevansky 2019, Krieger and Fiske 2006, and Greenwald and Krieger 2006.
33 See chapter 4.
34 Erickson 1996, Turco 2010, and Wingfield 2012.
35 Turco 2010 and Wingfield 2012.
36 US Department of the Interior, US Fish and Wildlife Service, and US Department of Commerce, US Census Bureau 2016.
37 Ho 2009 and Elting 2018.
38 Pao 2017, Kolhatkar 2014, and O'Donnell 2006.
39 Turco 2010 and Wingfield 2012, 2014.
40 Byrd 2017, Charles et al. 2009, and Espenshade and Radford 2009.
41 Ingraham 2014. See also Bonilla-Silva, Goar, and Embrick 2006.
42 US Commission on Civil Rights 2018 and Reardon 2016.
43 US Commission on Civil Rights 2018 and Reardon 2016.
44 Claytor 2020, Alba, Logan, and Stults 2000, Lacy 2007, and Bayer, Fang, and McMillan 2014.
45 Mouw and Entwisle 2006.
46 Cunningham 2020 and Khan 2010.
47 Hobbs 2014 and Williams 2011. See Woodson 2016b.
48 Beasley 2011.
49 Woodson 2016b.
50 Charles et al. 2009 and Torres and Charles 2004.
51 Martin, Tobin, and Spenner 2014.
52 Charles et al. 2009.
53 See Beasley 2012.
54 Chapter 2.
55 Armstrong and Hamilton 2013.
56 Graham 1999. Graham actually attended a public high school, but Brandon's point remains valid.
57 See Bourdieu 1984 and Erickson 1996.
58 Rivera 2015.

Chapter Four

1 Frank 2016.
2 Being staffed to such groups can be a double-edged sword. Professionals who hope to make partner at their firms may find that working in small practice groups dims their prospects of promotion because their firms may not see those departments as important growth areas.
3 Frank 2016.
4 Kanter 1977, 182.
5 Chapter 2.
6 Chapter 2.
7 There are countless examples of overstatements in the literature on Black pro-

fessionals, but the example perhaps most directly belied by their experiences is Msedale's assertion that "black female lawyers are not afforded the luxury of being comfortable in elite white law firms" (Melaku 2019, 43).

8 See Thompson 2014 and Yates 2012.

9 See Trawalter, Richeson, and Shelton 2009.

10 Bourdieu 1984, 1986.

11 Bourdieu 1984, 1986.

12 Bourdieu 1984 and Bonilla-Silva, Goar, and Embrick 2006.

13 Chapter 3.

14 Tyson 2011.

15 Chapter 1.

16 Jack 2019.

17 Jack 2019. The experiences of several of the Black professionals that I interviewed indicate that there are also substantial differences among the Black students who had attended prestigious prep schools (Jack's "privileged poor"), depending on the quality of their relationships with their White high school classmates.

18 Jack 2019.

19 See Alba, Logan, and Stults 2000.

20 Alba, Logan, and Stults 2000.

21 Clerge 2019.

22 The experiences of my interviewees are consistent with these theories. Most of the Black professionals with White familiarity hailed from middle-class households in White suburbs, and most interviewees who reported having at least one immigrant parent also exhibited perspectives consistent with White familiarity. However, those interviewees who grew up in predominantly Black neighborhoods or who developed predominantly non-White friendships as children and in college reported greater levels of racial discomfort. This pattern is consistent with the sociological theory of segmented assimilation. See Portes and Zhou 1993 and Neckerman, Carter, and Lee 1999.

23 Krieger and Sheldon 2015.

24 Bonilla-Silva 2003.

25 Black workers with White familiarity may be more aware of the difficulties of some White professionals in these firms because they have closer relationships with them.

Conclusion

1 Bonilla-Silva and Peoples 2022; Moore 2008, 2020; Ray 2019; and Evans and Moore 2015.

2 Rivera 2015, Turco 2010, Erickson 1996, Purcell 2013, and Friedman and Laurison 2019.

3   Dobbin and Kalev 2013. But see Kay and Gorman 2012.
4   Dobbin and Kalev 2016. See also Chang et al. 2019.
5   Dobbin and Kalev 2018 and Duguid and Thomas-Hunt 2015.
6   Pan 2020, Dobbin and Kalev 2016, and Forscher et al. 2019.
7   Merken 2021.
8   Scheiber and Eligon 2019.
9   Merken 2021.
10   Dobbin and Kalev 2016.
11   See King 2020.
12   *Parents Involved in Community Schools v. Seattle School District No. 1*, 551 U.S. 701 (2007).
13   Armstrong and Hamilton 2013.
14   Ross 2016.
15   Gurin 1999, Stearns, Buchmann, and Bonneau 2009, and Woodson 2016b.
16   Bonilla-Silva and Peoples 2022.
17   Bonilla-Silva and Peoples 2022.
18   See Woodson 2016b.
19   Harpalani 2017 and Keels 2020.
20   See Cain 2019.
21   Turco 2010, Erickson 1996, Purcell 2013, and Friedman and Laurison 2019.

Appendix A

1   Tansey 2007 and Biernacki and Waldorf 1981.
2   For these reasons, most large qualitative studies of Black professionals have used snowball or similar sampling methods. See Benjamin 2005, Feagin and Sikes 1995, Collins 1997, and Lacey 2007.
3   Further supporting the value of snowball sampling methods in this type of research, I sent a solicitation message to the administrators of several email listservs, including young Black alumni groups from several top-tier professional schools and the young alumni networks of two HBCU professional schools, but these outreach efforts yielded very few interviewees (eight in total).
4   Stephens 2007.
5   Wengraf 2001.
6   Oltmann 2016.
7   Sturges and Hanrahan 2004.
8   See Sturges and Hanrahan 2004.
9   Harvey 2011.
10   Oltmann 2016 and Sturges and Hanrahan 2004.
11   Sturges and Hanrahan 2004, Harvey 2011, and Vogl 2013.
12   Mendoza-Denton and Leiter 2018 and Wang, Stroebe, and Dovidio 2012.
13   Shepperd, Malone, and Sweeny 2008.

14   Ford 2008 and Crocker and Major 1989.
15   Osborne, Sengupta, and Sibley 2019 and McCoy and Major 2007.
16   Jost and Banaji 1994 and Owuamalam, Rubin, and Spears 2019.
17   Osborne, Sengupta, and Sibley 2019, Stroebe et al. 2010, and O'Brien and Major 2005.

References

Abelson, Max, and Bloomberg. 2021. "Goldman Sachs Reveals Black Workforce Numbers for the First Time." *Fortune*, April 20, 2021.

Abelson, Max, Sonali Basak, Kelsey Butler, Matthew Leising, Henny Surane, and Gillian Tan. 2020. "The Only One in the Room." *Bloomberg*, August 3, 2020.

Adediran, Atinuke O. 2018. "The Journey: Moving Racial Diversification Forward from Mere Commitment to Shared Value in Elite Law Firms." *International Journal of the Legal Profession* 25, no. 1 (January): 67–89.

Alba, Richard D., John R. Logan, and Brian J. Stults. 2000. "How Segregated Are Middle-Class African Americans?" *Social Problems* 47, no. 4 (November): 543–58.

Alcorn, Chauncey. 2021. "'Racial Bias Runs Deep' at America's Largest Banks, Study Says." *CNN*, March 18, 2021. https://www.cnn.com/2021/03/18/investing/bank-diversity-racial-bias-study/index.html.

Alden, William. 2014. "Wall Street's Young Bankers Are Still Mostly White and Male, Report Says." *New York Times*, September 30, 2014.

Alexander, Jeffrey C. 2004. "Cultural Pragmatics: Social Performance Between Ritual and Strategy." *Sociological Theory* 22, no. 4 (December): 527–73.

Algorani, Emad B., and Vikas Gupta. 2021. "Coping Mechanisms." In *StatPearls*. https://www.ncbi.nlm.nih.gov/books/NBK559031/.

Allport, Gordon. 1979. *The Nature of Prejudice*. 25th ed. New York: Basic Books.

Ambrogi, Bob. 2021. "Over Seven Years, Scant Progress in Law Firm Diversity, New Survey Shows." *LawSites*, August 17.

American Bar Association, Commission on Women in the Profession. 2018. *You Can't Change What You Can't See: Interrupting Racial and Gender Bias in the Legal Profession.* https://www.americanbar.org/products/ecd/ebk/358942050/.

Amis, John M., Johanna Mair, and Kamal A. Munir. 2020. "The Organizational Reproduction of Inequality." *Academy of Management Annals* 14, no. 1 (January): 195–230.

Anderson, Elijah. 1999. "The Social Situation of the Black Executive: Black and White Identities in the Corporate World." In *The Cultural Territories of Race: Black and White Boundaries,* edited by Michèlle Lamont, 3–29. Chicago: University of Chicago Press.

Anderson, Elijah. 2015. "The White Space." *Sociology of Race and Ethnicity* 1, no. 1: 10–21.

Anderson, Monica. 2018. *Black STEM Employees Perceive a Range of Race-Related Slights and Inequities at Work.* Pew Research Center. January 10.

Armstrong, Elizabeth A., and Laura T. Hamilton. 2013. *Paying for the Party: How College Maintains Inequality.* Cambridge, MA: Harvard University Press.

Aron, Arthur, and Natalie Nardone. 2012. "Self and Close Relationships." In *Handbook of Self and Identity,* edited by Mark R. Leary and June Price Tangney, 520–41. New York: Guilford Press.

Ashley, Wendy. 2014. "The Angry Black Woman: The Impact of Pejorative Stereotypes on Psychotherapy with Black Women." *Social Work in Public Health* 29, no. 1 (November): 27–34.

Bain & Company. 2021. *Our Journey: 2021 Diversity, Equity, and Inclusion Report.* Accessed October 17, 2022. https://www.bain.com/globalassets/noindex/2021/ bain_report_diversity_equity_and_inclusion_2021.pdf.

Baldi, Stéphane, and Debra Branch McBrier. 1997. "Do the Determinants of Promotion Differ for Blacks and Whites? Evidence from the U.S. Labor Market." *Work and Occupations* 24, no. 4 (November): 478–97.

Banaji, Mahzarin R., and Anthony G. Greenwald. 2016. *Blindspot: Hidden Biases of Good People.* New York: Bantam Books.

Banks, Erik. 2004. *Working the Street: What You Need to Know about Life on Wall Street.* New York: St. Martin's Press.

Baron, James N., and Jeffrey Pfeffer. 1994. "The Social Psychology of Organizations and Inequality." *Social Psychology Quarterly* 57, no. 3 (September): 190–209.

Bayer, Patrick, Hanming Fang, and Robert McMillan. 2014. "*Separate*

When Equal? Racial Inequality and Residential Segregation." *Journal of Urban Economics* 82 (July): 32–48.

BBC News. 2017. "Implicit Bias: Is Everyone Racist?" June 5, 2017. https://www.bbc.com/news/magazine-40124781.

Beasley, Maya A. 2012. *Opting Out? Losing the Potential of America's Young Black Elite.* Chicago: University of Chicago Press.

Benjamin, Lois. 2005. *The Black Elite: Still Facing the Color Line in the Twenty-first Century.* 2nd ed. Lanham, MD: Rowman & Littlefield.

Bergsieker, Hilary B., Lisa M. Leslie, Vanessa S. Constantine, and Susan T. Fiske. 2012. "Stereotyping by Omission: Eliminate the Negative, Accentuate the Positive." *Journal of Personality and Social Psychology* 102, no. 6 (March): 1214–38.

Bertrand, Marianne, and Sendhil Mullainathan. 2004. "Are Emily and Greg More Employable than Lakisha and Jamal? A Field Experiment on Labor Market Discrimination." *American Economic Review* 94, no. 4 (September): 991–1013.

Bielby, William T. 2011. "Minority Vulnerability in Privileged Occupations: Why Do African American Financial Advisers Earn Less than Whites in a Large Financial Services Firm?" *ANNALS of the American Academy of Political and Social Science* 639, no. 1 (December): 13–32.

Biernacki, Patrick, and Dan Waldorf. 1981. "Snowball Sampling: Problems and Techniques of Chain Referral Sampling." *Sociological Methods & Research* 10, no. 2 (November): 141–63.

Blair, Irene V., Charles M. Judd, Melody S. Sadler, and Christopher Jenkins. 2002. "The Role of Afrocentric Features in Person Perception: Judging by Features and Categories." *Journal of Personality and Social Psychology* 83, no. 1 (July): 5–25.

Bodenhausen, Galen V., Andrew R. Todd, and Jennifer A. Richeson. 2009. "Controlling Prejudice and Stereotyping: Antecedents, Mechanisms, and Contexts." In *Handbook of Prejudice, Stereotyping, and Discrimination,* edited by Todd D. Nelson, 111–35. New York: Psychology Press.

Bonilla-Silva, Eduardo. 2003. *Racism without Racists: Color-Blind Racism and the Persistence of Racial Inequality in the United States.* Lanham, MD: Rowman & Littlefield.

Bonilla-Silva, Eduardo, Carla Goar, and David G. Embrick. 2006. "When Whites Flock Together: The Social Psychology of White Habitus." *Critical Sociology* 32, nos. 2–3 (March): 229–53.

Bonilla-Silva, Eduardo, and Crystal E. Peoples. 2022. "Historically White Colleges and Universities: The Unbearable Whiteness of (Most) Colleges and Universities in America." *American Behavioral Scientist* 66, no. 11 (January): 1–15.

Bos, Arjan E. R., John B. Pryor, Glenn D. Reeder, and Sarah E. Stutterheim. 2013. "Stigma: Advances in Theory and Research." *Basic and Applied Social Psychology* 35, no. 1 (February): 1–9.

Bourdieu, Pierre. 1984. *Distinction: A Social Critique of the Judgment of Taste*. Cambridge, MA: Harvard University Press.

———. 1986. "The Forms of Capital." In *Handbook of Theory and Research for the Sociology of Education*, edited by John G. Richardson, 47–48. New York: Greenwood Press.

Braxton, Greg. 1998. "For Many Black Viewers, 'Seinfeld's' End Is Nonevent." *Los Angeles Times*, May 12, 1998.

Brewer, Marilynn B. 2001. "Ingroup Identification and Intergroup Conflict: When Does Ingroup Love Become Outgroup Hate?" In *Social Identity, Intergroup Conflict, and Conflict Reduction*, edited by Richard D. Ashmore, Lee J. Jussim, and David Wilder, 17–41. New York: Oxford University Press.

———. 2002. "The Psychology of Prejudice: Ingroup Love or Outgroup Hate?" *Journal of Social Issues* 55, no. 3 (December): 429–44.

Brock, André. 2012. "From the Blackhand Side: Twitter as a Cultural Conversation." *Journal of Broadcasting & Electronic Media* 56, no. 4 (December): 529–49.

Business Today. 2018. "Facebook's 'Things in Common' Feature Lets You Make Friends with Strangers." August 27, 2018. https://www .businesstoday.in/technology/news/story/facebook-things-common -feature-lets-you-friends-strangers-109054-2018-08-27.

Byrd, W. Carson. 2017. *Poison in the Ivy: Race Relations and the Reproduction of Inequality on Elite College Campuses*. New Brunswick, NJ: Rutgers University Press.

Cain, Carol. 2019. "Detroit Woman a Leader in Merger Creating Giant Minority-Owned Investment Bank in US." *Detroit Free Press*, October 12, 2019.

Capers, Bennett. 2021. "The Law School as a White Space." *Minnesota Law Review* 106: 7.

Cappeli, Peter, and Anna Tavis. 2016. "The Performance Management Revolution." *Harvard Business Review* (October). https://hbr.org/2016/ 10/the-performance-management-revolution.

Carbado, Devon W., and Mitu Gulati. 1999. "Working Identity." *Cornell Law Review* 85, no. 5 (July): 1259–1308.

—————. 2001. "The Fifth Black Woman." *Journal of Contemporary Legal Issues* 11 (January): 701–29.

—————. 2013. *Acting White? Rethinking Race in Post-Racial America.* New York: Oxford University Press.

Carter, Prudence. 2003. "'Black' Cultural Capital, Status Positioning, and Schooling Conflicts for Low-Income African American Youth." *Social Problems* 50, no. 1: 136–55.

Casad, Bettina J., Zachary W. Petzel, and Emily A. Ingalls. 2019. "A Model of Threatening Academic Environments Predicts Women STEM Majors' Self-Esteem and Engagement in STEM." *Sex Roles* 80 (April): 469–88.

Castilla, Emilio J. 2008. "Gender, Race, and Meritocracy in Organizational Careers." *American Journal of Sociology* 113, no. 6 (May): 1479–1526.

CBS News. 2018. "CBS News Asks: What Is America's Favorite Music Genre?" January 28, 2018. https://www.cbsnews.com/news/cbs-news -asks-what-is-americas-favorite-music-genre/.

Chambers Associate. 2021. "Top Law Firms for Diversity." https://www .chambers-associate.com/law-firms/associate-satisfaction-surveys/the -best-firms-for-diversity.

Chan, Curtis K., and Michel Anteby. 2016. "Task Segregation as a Mechanism for Within-Job Inequality: Women and Men of the Transportation Security Administration." *Administrative Science Quarterly* 61, no. 2 (June): 184–216.

Chang, Edward H., Katherine L. Milkman, Laura J. Zarrow, Kasandra Brabaw, Dena M. Gromet, Reb Rebele, Cade Massey, Angela L. Duckworth, and Adam Grant. 2019. "Does Diversity Training Work the Way It's Supposed To?" *Harvard Business Review*, July 9, 2019. https:// hbr.org/2019/07/does-diversity-training-work-the-way-its-supposed -to.

Charles, Camille Zubrinsky, Mary J. Fischer, Margarita A. Mooney, and Douglas S. Massey. 2009. *Taming the River: Negotiating the Academic, Financial, and Social Currents in Selective Colleges and Universities.* Princeton, NJ: Princeton University Press.

Chen, Ruiqi. 2021. "Coke GC Tired of 'Good Intentions,' Wants Firm Diversity Now." *Bloomberg News*, January 28, 2021. https://news .bloomberglaw.com/business-and-practice/coke-gc-tired-of-good -intentions-wants-law-firm-diversity-now.

Chen, Vivia. 2019. "Am Law Firms with Zero Black Partners—How Is This Possible in 2019?" *American Lawyer*, June 6, 2019. https://www

.law.com/americanlawyer/2019/06/06/am-law-firms-with-zero-black
-partners-how-is-this-possible-in-2019/.

Claytor, Cassi Pittman. 2020. *Black Privilege: Modern Middle-Class Blacks with Credentials and Cash to Spend*. Stanford, CA: Stanford University Press.

Clerge, Orly. 2019. *The New Noir: Race, Identity & Diaspora in Black Suburbia*. Oakland: University of California Press.

Cohan, William D. 2018. "Wall Street Is Still a 'White Man's World' with a 'Veneer of Diversity.'" *CNBC*, March 14, 2018. https://www.cnbc .com/2018/03/13/wall-street-diversity-efforts-have-a-long-way-to-go -commentary.html.

Collins, Nancy L., and Lynn Carol Miller. 1994. "Self-Disclosure and Liking: A Meta-analytic Review." *Psychological Bulletin* 116, no. 3 (November): 457–75.

Collins, Sharon M. 1997. *Black Corporate Executives: The Making or Breaking of a Black Middle Class*. Philadelphia: Temple University Press.

Collins, Todd A., Tao L. Dumas, and Laura P. Moyer. 2017. "Intersecting Disadvantages: Race, Gender, and Age Discrimination among Attorneys." *Social Science Quarterly* 98, no. 5 (February): 1642–58.

Correll, Shelley J., Katherine R. Weisshaar, Alison T. Wynn, and JoAnne Delfino Wehner. 2020. "Inside the Black Box of Organizational Life: The Gendered Language of Performance Assessment." *American Sociological Review* 85, no. 6 (December): 1022–50.

Crocker, Jennifer, and Brenda Major. 1989. "Social Stigma and Self-Esteem: The Self-Protective Properties of Stigma." *Psychological Review* 96, no. 4 (October): 608–30.

Crocker, Jennifer, Brenda Major, and Claude Steele. 2010. "Social Stigma." In *Handbook of Social Psychology*, vol. 2, edited by Susan T. Fiske, Daniel T. Gilbert, and Gardner Lindzey, 504–53. Hoboken, NJ: Wiley.

Crocker, Jennifer, Kristin Voelkl, Maria Testa, and Brenda Major. 1991. "Social Stigma: The Affective Consequences of Attributional Ambiguity." *Journal of Personality and Social Psychology* 60, no. 2 (February): 218–28.

Cuddy, Amy J. C., Susan T. Fiske, Virginia S. Y. Kwan, Peter Glick, Stéphanie Demoulin, Jacques-Philippe Leyens, Michael Harris Bond, Jean-Claude Croizet, Naomi Ellemers, Ed Sleebos, Tin Tin Htun, Hyun-Jeong Kim, Greg Maio, Judi Perry, Kristina Petkova, Valery Todorov, Rosa Rodríguez-Bailón, Elena Morales, Miguel Moya, Marisol Palacios, Vanessa Smith, Rolando Perez, Jorge Vala, and Rene

Ziegler. 2009. "Stereotype Content Model Across Cultures: Towards Universal Similarities and Some Differences." *British Journal of Social Psychology* 48, no. 1 (January): 1–33.

Culver, Leslie P. 2018. "Conscious Identity Performance." *San Diego Law Review* 55 (October): 577–616.

Cunningham, Vinson. 2020. "Test Case: Prep for Prep and the Fault Lines in New York's Schools." *New Yorker*, March 9, 2020.

Currid-Halkett, Elizabeth. 2017. *The Sum of Small Things: A Theory of the Aspirational Class*. Princeton, NJ: Princeton University Press.

Devine, Patricia G. 1989. "Stereotypes and Prejudice: Their Automatic and Controlled Components." *Journal of Personality and Social Psychology* 56, no. 1 (January): 5–18.

Diaz, Luis J., and Patrick C. Dunican Jr. 2011. "Ending the Revolving Door Syndrome in Law." *Seton Hall Law Review* 41, no. 3 (November): 947–1003.

DiMaggio, Paul. 1987. "Classification in Art." *American Sociological Review* 52, no. 4 (August): 440–55.

Dinovitzer, Ronit, and Bryant Garth. 2020. "The New Place of Corporate Law Firms in the Structuring of Elite Legal Careers." *Law & Social Inquiry* 45, no. 2 (May): 339–71.

DiTomaso, Nancy. 2013. *The American Non-Dilemma: Racial Inequality without Racism*. New York: Russell Sage Foundation.

Diversity Lab. 2021. "Inclusion Blueprint." https://www.diversitylab.com/research/inclusion-blueprint/.

Dobbin, Frank, and Alexandra Kalev. 2013. "The Origins and Effects of Corporate Diversity Training Programs." In *The Oxford Handbook of Diversity and Work*, edited by Quinetta M. Roberson, 253–81. New York: Oxford University Press.

———. 2016. "Why Diversity Programs Fail." *Harvard Business Review* (July–August). https://hbr.org/2016/07/why-diversity-programs-fail.

———. 2018. "Why Doesn't Diversity Training Work?" *Anthropology Now* 10, no. 2 (September): 48–55.

Donovan, Karen. 2006. "Pushed by Clients, Law Firms Step Up Diversity Efforts." *New York Times*, July 21. https://www.nytimes.com/2006/07/21/business/21legal.html.

Dorrian, Patrick. 2022. "Davis Polk Job Bias Evidence Warrants Trial, Black Lawyer Says." *Bloomberg Law*, February 7, 2022. https://news.bloomberglaw.com/litigation/davis-polk-black-ex-lawyer-says-evidence-warrants-job-bias-trial.

Doss, Richard C., and Alan M. Gross. 1994. "The Effects of Black English and Code-Switching on Intraracial Perceptions." *Journal of Black Psychology* 20, no. 3 (August): 282–93.

Dovidio, John F., Nancy Evans, and Richard B. Tyler. 1986. "Racial Stereotypes: The Content of Their Cognitive Representations." *Journal of Experimental Social Psychology* 22, no. 1 (January): 22–37.

Dovidio, John F., Miles Hewstone, Peter Glick, and Victoria M. Esses. 2010. "Prejudice, Stereotyping and Discrimination: Theoretical and Empirical Overview." In *The SAGE Handbook of Prejudice, Stereotyping, and Discrimination*, edited by John F. Dovidio, 5. Boston: Credo Reference.

Duguid, Michelle M., and Melissa C. Thomas-Hunt. 2015. "Condoning Stereotyping? How Awareness of Stereotyping Prevalence Impacts Expression of Stereotypes." *Journal of Applied Psychology* 100, no. 2: 343–59.

Dumas, Tracy L., Katherine W. Phillips, and Nancy P. Rothbard. 2013. "Getting Closer at the Company Party: Integration Experiences, Racial Dissimilarity, and Workplace Relationships." *Organization Science* 24, no. 5: 1377–1401.

Dunn, Amina. 2019. *Younger, College-Educated Black Americans Are Most Likely to Feel Need to "Code-Switch."* Pew Research Center. September 24. https://www.pewresearch.org/fact-tank/2019/09/24/younger-college-educated-black-americans-are-most-likely-to-feel-need-to-code-switch/.

Dupree, Cydney H., and Susan T. Fiske. 2019. "Self-Presentation in Interracial Settings: The Competence Downshift by White Liberals." *Journal of Personality and Social Psychology* 117, no. 3 (September): 579–604.

Elting, Liz. 2018. "How to Navigate a Boys' Club Culture." *Forbes*, July 27, 2018. https://www.forbes.com/sites/lizelting/2018/07/27/how-to-navigate-a-boys-club-culture/.

Erickson, B. H. 1996. "Culture, Class, and Connections." *American Journal of Sociology* 102, no. 1 (July 1996): 217–51.

Espenshade, Thomas J., and Alexandria Walton Radford. 2009. *No Longer Separate, Not Yet Equal: Race and Class in Elite College Admissions and Campus Life*. Princeton, NJ: Princeton University Press.

Evans, Louwanda. 2013. *Cabin Pressure: African American Pilots, Flight Attendants, and Emotional Labor*. Lanham, MD: Rowman & Littlefield.

Evans, Louwanda, and Wendy Leo Moore. 2015. "Impossible Burdens:

White Institutions, Emotional Labor, and Micro-Resistance." *Social Problems* 62, no. 3 (August): 439–54.

Feagin, Joe R. 1991. "The Continuing Significance of Race: Antiblack Discrimination in Public Places." *American Sociological Review* 56, no. 1 (February): 101–16.

Feagin, Joe R., and Melvin P. Sikes. 1995. *Living with Racism: The Black Middle-Class Experience.* Boston: Beacon Press.

Fiske, Susan T. 2012. "Warmth and Competence: Stereotype Content Issues for Clinicians and Researchers." *Canadian Psychology* 53, no. 1 (February): 14–20.

Fiske, Susan T., Amy J. C. Cuddy, Peter Glick, and Jun Xu. 2002. "A Model of (Often Mixed) Stereotype Content: Competence and Warmth Respectively Follow From Perceived Status and Competition." *Journal of Personality and Social Psychology* 82, no. 6 (June): 878–902.

Flock, Elizabeth. 2013. "Poll: White Americans Far Less Likely to Have Friends of Another Race." *U.S. News & World Report.* August 8, 2013. https://www.usnews.com/news/articles/2013/08/08/poll-white -americans-far-less-likely-to-have-friends-of-another-race.

Folkman, Susan, and Judith Tedlie Moskowitz. 2004. "Coping: Pitfalls and Promise." *Annual Review of Psychology* 55 (February): 745–74.

Ford, Richard Thompson. 2008. *The Race Card: How Bluffing about Bias Makes Race Relations Worse.* New York: Farrar, Straus, and Giroux.

Forscher, Patrick S., Calvin K. Lai, Jordan R. Axt, Charles R. Ebersole, Michelle Herman, Patricia G. Devine, and Brian A. Nosek. 2019. "Meta-Analysis of Procedures to Change Implicit Measures." *Journal of Personality and Social Psychology* 117, no. 3 (September): 522–59.

Frank, Robert. 2016. *Success and Luck: Good Fortune and the Myth of Meritocracy.* Princeton, NJ: Princeton University Press.

Friedman, Sam, and Daniel Laurison. 2019. *The Class Ceiling: Why It Pays to Be Privileged.* Bristol: Policy Press.

Gaddis, S. Michael. 2015. "Discrimination in the Credential Society: An Audit Study of Race and College Selectivity in the Labor Market." *Social Forces* 93, no. 4 (June): 1451–79.

Galanter, Marc, and William D. Henderson. 2007. "The Elastic Tournament: A Second Transformation of the Big Law Firm." *Stanford Law Review* 60, no. 6 (April): 1867–1929.

Garth, Bryant G., and Joyce S. Sterling. 2018. "Diversity, Hierarchy, and Fit in Legal Careers: Insights from Fifteen Years of Qualitative Interviews." *Georgetown Journal of Legal Ethics* 31, no. 1 (Winter): 123–74.

Gellhorn, Ernest. 1968. "The Law Schools and the Negro." *Duke Law Journal* 17, no. 6 (December): 1069–99.

Godsil, Rachel D., and L. Song Richardson. 2017. "Racial Anxiety." *Iowa Law Review* 102, no. 5 (July): 2235–63.

Goffman, Erving. 1963. *Stigma: Notes on the Management of Spoiled Identity*. New York: Simon & Schuster.

Gracian, Mack. 1996. "The Top 25 Blacks on Wall Street." *Black Enterprise*, October 1, 1996.

Graham, Lawrence Otis. 1999. *Our Kind of People: Inside America's Black Upper Class*. New York: HarperCollins.

Green, Tristin K. 2005. "Work Culture and Discrimination." *California Law Review* 93, no. 3 (May): 623–84.

Green, Tristin K., and Alexandra Kalev. 2007. "Discrimination-Reducing Measures at the Relational Level." *Hastings Law Journal* 59, no. 6 (June): 1435–61.

Greene, D. Wendy. 2008. "Title VII: What's Hair (and Other Race-Based Characteristics) Got to Do with It?" *University of Colorado Law Review* 79, no. 4 (December): 1355–94.

Greenwald, Anthony G., and Lisa Hamilton Krieger. 2006. "Implicit Bias: Scientific Foundations." *California Law Review* 94, no. 4 (July): 945–67.

Gulati, Mitu, and David B. Wilkins. 1996. "Why Are There So Few Black Lawyers in Corporate Law Firms? An Institutional Analysis." *California Law Review* 84, no. 3 (May): 493–625.

Gurin, Patricia. 1999. "Expert Report of Patricia Gurin." *Michigan Journal of Race and Law* 5, no. 1: 363–425.

Hall, Erika V., Alison V. Hall, Adam D. Galinsky, and Katherine W. Phillips. 2019. "MOSAIC: A Model of Stereotyping through Associated and Intersectional Categories." *Academy of Management Review* 44, no. 3 (July): 643–72.

Harpalani, Vinay. 2017. "'Safe Spaces' and the Educational Benefits of Diversity." *Duke Journal of Constitutional Law & Public Policy* 13, no. 1 (March): 117–66.

Harvey, William S. 2011. "Strategies for Conducting Elite Interviews." *Qualitative Research* 11, no. 4: 431–41. http://doi.org/10.1177/1468794111404329.

Hauser, Christine. 2018. "How Professionals of Color Say They Counter Bias at Work." *New York Times*, December 12, 2018. https://www.nytimes.com/2018/12/12/us/racial-bias-work.html.

Henkel, Kristin E., John F. Dovidio, and Samuel L. Gaertner. 2006. "Institutional Discrimination, Individual Racism, and Hurricane Katrina." *Analyses of Social Issues and Public Policy* 6, no. 1 (December): 99–124.

Hester, Neil, and Kurt Gray. 2018. "For Black Men, Being Tall Increases Threat Stereotyping and Police Stops." *PNAS* 115, no. 11 (March): 2711–15.

Hewlett, Sylvia Ann. 2013. *(Forget a Mentor) Find a Sponsor: The New Way to Fast-Track Your Career.* Cambridge, MA: Harvard Business Review Press.

Hewstone, Miles, Mark Rubin, and Hazel Willis. 2002. "Intergroup Bias." *Annual Review of Psychology* 53 (February): 575–604.

Higginbotham, Evelyn, and Lynn Weber. 1999. "Perceptions of Workplace Discrimination among Black and White Managerial Women." In *Latina and African-American Women at Work: Race, Gender, and Economic Inequality,* edited by Irene Brown, 334. New York: Russell Sage Foundation.

Hinshaw, Stephen P. 2007. *The Mark of Shame: Stigma of Mental Illness and an Agenda for Change.* New York: Oxford University Press.

Ho, Karen. 2009. *Liquidated: An Ethnography of Wall Street.* Durham, NC: Duke University Press.

Hobbs, Jeff. 2014. *The Short and Tragic Life of Robert Peace: A Brilliant Young Man Who Left Newark for the Ivy League.* New York: Scribner.

Hunger, Jeffrey M., and Brenda Major. 2014. "Weight Stigma Mediates the Association between BMI and Self-Reported Health." *Health Psychology* 34, no. 2 (August): 172–75.

Hunt, Matthew O. 2007. "African American, Hispanic, and White Beliefs about Black/White Inequality, 1977–2004." *American Sociological Review* 72, no. 3 (June): 390–415.

Ingraham, Christopher. 2014. "Three Quarters of Whites Don't Have Any Non-white Friends." *Washington Post,* August 25, 2014. https://www.washingtonpost.com/news/wonk/wp/2014/08/25/three-quarters-of-whites-dont-have-any-non-white-friends/.

Inzlicht, Michael, Joshua Aronson, Catherine Good, and Linda McKay. 2006. "A Particular Resiliency to Threatening Environments." *Journal of Experimental Social Psychology* 42, no. 3 (May): 323–36.

Inzlicht, Michael, Joshua Aronson, and Rodolfo Mendoza-Denton. 2009. "On Being the Target of Prejudice: Educational Implications." In *Coping with Minority Status: Responses to Exclusion and Inclusion,* edited by

Fabrizio Butera and John M. Levine, 13–36. Cambridge: Cambridge University Press.

Inzlicht, Michael, and Catherine Good. 2006. "How Environments Threaten Academic Performance, Self-Knowledge, and Sense of Belonging." In *Stigma and Group Inequality: Social Psychological Approaches*, edited by Shana Levin and Colette van Laar, 129–50. Mahwah, NJ: Erlbaum.

Jack, Anthony Abraham. 2019. *The Privileged Poor: How Elite Colleges Are Failing Disadvantaged Students*. Cambridge, MA: Harvard University Press.

Jackson, Dylan, and Justin Henry. 2021. "Despite All That Happened Last Year, Many Law Firms Still Have No Black Partners." *American Lawyer*, May 25, 2021. https://www.law.com/americanlawyer/2021/05/25/despite-all-that-happened-last-year-many-law-firms-still-have-no-black-partners/.

Jackson, Liane. 2016. "Minority Women Are Disappearing from BigLaw—and Here's Why." *ABA Journal*, March 1. https://www.abajournal.com/magazine/article/minority_women_are_disappearing_from_biglaw_and_heres_why.

James, Erika Hayes. 2000. "Race-Related Differences in Promotions and Support: Underlying Effects of Human and Social Capital." *Organization Science* 11, no. 5 (September–October): 493–508.

Jet. 1997. "How Blacks Differ from Whites in TV Show Choices." March 17, 1997.

Jones, Christopher P. 1987. "Stigma: Tattooing and Branding in Graeco-Roman Antiquity." *Journal of Roman Studies* 77 (November): 139–55.

Jost, John T., and Mahzarin R. Banaji. 1994. "The Role of Stereotyping in System-Justification and the Production of False Consciousness." *British Journal of Social Psychology* 33, no. 1 (March): 1–27. https://doi.org/10.1111/j.2044-8309.1994.tb01008.

Joyner, Kara, and Grace Kao. 2000. "School Racial Composition and Adolescent Racial Homophily." *Social Science Quarterly* 81, no. 3 (September): 810–25.

JPMorgan Chase & Co. 2021. *2020 Workforce Composition Disclosure*. https://www.jpmorganchase.com/content/dam/jpmc/jpmorgan-chase-and-co/documents/workforce-composition-disclosure.pdf.

Just Drinks. 2017. "Cognac's Ethnic Division in the US—Focus." Analysis, January 6. https://www.just-drinks.com/features/cognacs-ethnic-division-in-the-us-focus/.

Kang, Jerry. 2005. "Trojan Horses of Race." *Harvard Law Review* 118, no. 5 (March): 1489–1593.

Kanter, Rosabeth Moss. 1977. *Men and Women of the Corporation*. New York: Basic Books.

Kay, Fiona M., and Elizabeth H. Gorman. 2012. "Developmental Practices, Organizational Culture, and Minority Representation in Organizational Leadership: The Case of Partners in Large U.S. Law Firms." *ANNALS of the American Academy of Political and Social Science* 639, no. 1 (January): 91–113.

Keels, Micere. 2020. *Campus Counterspaces: Black and Latinx Students' Search for Community at Historically White Universities*. Ithaca, NY: Cornell University Press.

Khan, Shamus Rahman. 2010. *Privilege: The Making of an Elite at the St. Paul's School*. Princeton, NJ: Princeton University Press.

King, Marissa. 2020. *Social Chemistry: Decoding the Patterns of Human Connection*. New York: Dutton.

Knox, Liam. 2019. "All-Black H.S. Team's Success Highlights Golf's Problem with Diversity." *NBC News*, December 12, 2019. https://www.nbcnews.com/news/nbcblk/all-black-high-school-team-s-success-highlights-golf-s-n1100021.

Kolhatkar, Sheelah. 2014. "A Lawsuit Peeks Inside the Goldman Sachs 'Boys' Club.'" *Bloomberg*, July 2, 2014. https://www.bloomberg.com/news/articles/2014-07-02/a-lawsuit-peeks-inside-the-goldman-sachs-boys-club.

Kossinets, Gueorgi, and Duncan J. Watts. 2009. "Origins of Homophily in an Evolving Social Network." *American Journal of Sociology* 115, no. 2 (March): 405–50.

Krieger, Lawrence S., and Kennon M. Sheldon. 2015. "What Makes Lawyers Happy? A Data-Driven Prescription to Redefine Professional Success." *George Washington Law Review* 83, no. 2: 554–626.

Krieger, Linda Hamilton, and Susan T. Fiske. 2006. "Behavioral Realism." *California Law Review* 94, no. 4 (July): 997–1062.

Lacy, Karyn R. 2007. *Blue-Chip Black: Race, Class, and Status in the New Black Middle Class*. Berkeley: University of California Press.

Lamont, Michèle, and Annette Lareau. 1988. "Cultural Capital: Allusions, Gaps and Glissandos in Recent Theoretical Developments." *Sociological Theory* 6, no. 2 (Autumn): 153–68.

Lamont, Michèle, Graziella Moraes Silva, Jessica Welburn, Joshua Guetzkow, Nissim Mizrachi, Hanna Herzog, and Elisa Reis. 2019. *Getting*

Respect: Responding to Stigma and Discrimination in the United States, Brazil, and Israel. Princeton, NJ: Princeton University Press.

Lazarsfeld, Paul F., and Robert K. Merton. 1954. "Friendship as a Social Process: A Substantive and Methodological Analysis." In *Freedom and Control in Modern Society*, edited by Morroe Berger, Theodore Abel, and Charles H. Page, 18. New York: D. Van Nostrand.

Leong, Nancy. 2013. "Racial Capitalism." *Harvard Law Review* 126, no. 8 (June): 2151–2226.

Levin, Gary. 2017. "Who's Watching What: TV Shows Ranked by Racial and Ethnic Groups." *USA Today*, June 27, 2017. https://www.usatoday.com/story/life/tv/2017/06/27/whos-watching-what-tv-shows-ranked-racial-and-ethnic-groups/103199848/.

Levit, Nancy. 2011. "Lawyers Suing Law Firms: The Limits on Attorney Employment Discrimination Claims and the Prospects for Creating Happy Lawyers." *University of Pittsburgh Law Review* 73, no. 1: 65–106.

Lewis, Amanda E., and John B. Diamond. 2015. *Despite the Best Intentions: How Racial Inequality Thrives in Good Schools.* New York: Oxford University Press.

Lewis, Robin J., Valerian J. Derlega, Jessica L. Griffin, and Alison C. Krowinski. 2003. "Stressors for Gay Men and Lesbians: Life Stress, Gay-Related Stress, Stigma Consciousness, and Depressive Symptoms." *Journal of Social and Clinical Psychology* 22, no. 6 (December): 716–29.

Libling, Joshia. 2020. "Up or Out: Why Litigation Associates Need to Make a Decision by Their Fourth Year." *American Lawyer*, June 29, 2020. https://www.law.com/americanlawyer/2020/06/29/up-or-out-why-litigation-associates-need-to-make-a-decision-by-their-fourth-year/.

Link, Bruce G., and Jo C. Phelan. 2001. "Conceptualizing Stigma." *Annual Review of Sociology* 27 (August): 363–85.

Loury, Glenn C. 2003. *The Anatomy of Racial Stigma.* Cambridge, MA: Harvard University Press.

Lublin, Joann S. 2021. "Employee Resource Groups Are on the Rise at U.S. Companies." *Wall Street Journal*, October 31, 2021. https://www.wsj.com/articles/why-ergs-are-on-the-rise-11635532232?mod=djem10point.

Major, Brenda, and Laurie T. O'Brien. 2005. "The Social Psychology of Stigma." *Annual Review of Psychology* 56 (February): 393–421.

Major, Lindsey & Africa. 2017. *Minding the Gap: Do Today's Associates Defy Generational Stereotypes?* Above the Law. April. https://

info.abovethelaw.com/mla-millennial-report?utm_campaign=
MLA%20Millennial%20Report&utm_source=MLA%20Millenial
%20Report&utm_medium=Report&_ga=2.201013930.525744530
.1650888952-2060211305.1649762490.

Mark, Noah P. 2003. "Culture and Competition: Homophily and Distancing Explanations for Cultural Niches." *American Sociological Review* 68, no. 3 (June): 319–45.

Mark, Noah P., and Daniel H. Harris. 2012. "Roommates' Race and Racial Composition of White College Students' Ego Networks." *Social Science Research* 41, no. 2: 331–42.

Martin, Nathan D., William Tobin, and Kenneth I. Spenner. 2014. "Interracial Friendships across the College Years: Evidence from a Longitudinal Case Study." *Journal of College Student Development* 55, no. 7 (October): 720–25.

Massen, Jorg J. M., and Sonja E. Koski. 2014. "Chimps of a Feather Sit Together: Chimpanzee Friendships Are Based on Homophily in Personality." *Evolution and Human Behavior* 35, no. 1 (January): 1–8.

May, Reuben A. Buford. 2014. *Urban Nightlife: Entertaining Race, Class, and Culture in Public Space.* New Brunswick, NJ: Rutgers University Press.

McCoy, Shannon K., and Brenda Major. 2007. "Priming Meritocracy and the Psychological Justification of Inequality." *Journal of Experimental Social Psychology* 43, no. 3 (May): 341–51.

McCluney, Courtney L., Kathrina Robotham, Serenity Lee, Richard Smith, and Myles Durkee. 2019. "The Costs of Code-Switching." *Harvard Business Review*, November 15, 2019. https://hbr.org/2019/11/the -costs-of-codeswitching.

McElhaney, Alicia. 2020. "Consulting Firms Are Overwhelmingly White, Data Show." *Institutional Investor*, December 10, 2020. https://www .institutionalinvestor.com/article/b1plyvx3pjzw6d/Consulting-Firms -Are-Overwhelmingly-White-Data-Show.

McGregor, Jena. 2013. "The Corporate Kabuki of Performance Reviews." *Washington Post*, February 14, 2013. https://www.washingtonpost .com/national/on-leadership/the-corporate-kabuki-of-performance -reviews/2013/02/14/59b60e86-7624-11e2-aa12-e6cf1d31106b_story .html.

McLymore, Arriana. 2020. "Black Male Lawyers Detail Racial Bias Inside and Outside Big Law." *Westlaw Today*, October 19, 2020. https://today

.westlaw.com/Document/I36ad56d0122d11eb9a61f379d51e970c/View/FullText.html?transitionType=Default&contextData=(sc.Default).

McLymore, Arriana, and Caroline Spiezio. 2021. "Law Firm Diversity Chiefs Gain Numbers-and Influence." Reuters, July 7. https://www.reuters.com/legal/legalindustry/law-firm-diversity-chiefs-gain-numbers-influence-2021-07-07/.

McPherson, Miller, Lynn Smith-Lovin, and James M. Cook. 2001. "Birds of a Feather: Homophily in Social Networks." *Annual Review of Sociology* 27 (August): 415–44.

Melaku, Tsedale M. 2019. *You Don't Look Like a Lawyer: Black Women and Systemic Gendered Racism.* Lanham, MD: Rowman & Littlefield.

Mendoza-Denton, Rodolfo, Geraldine Downey, Valerie J. Purdie, Angelina Davis, and Janina Pietrzak. 2002. "Sensitivity to Status-Based Rejection: Implications for African American Students' College Experience." *Journal of Personality and Social Psychology* 83, no. 4 (October): 896–918.

Mendoza-Denton, Rodolfo, and Jordan B. Leiter. 2018. "Stigma, Health, and Individual Differences." In *The Oxford Handbook of Stigma, Discrimination, and Health,* edited by Brenda Major, John F. Dovidio, and Bruce G. Link, 384. New York: Oxford University Press.

Merken, Sara. 2021. "New Law Firm Commitments Include Goal That Ties Partner Pay to Diversity." Reuters, September 30. https://www.reuters.com/legal/legalindustry/new-law-firm-commitments-include-goal-that-ties-partner-pay-diversity-2021-09-30/.

Merle, Renae, and Jena McGregor. 2019. "Wall Street Says It Cares about Diversity: But Most Big Banks Won't Share Complete Workforce Data." *Washington Post,* December 6, 2019. https://www.washingtonpost.com/business/2019/12/06/wall-street-says-it-cares-about-diversity-most-big-banks-wont-share-complete-workforce-data/.

Methot, Jessica R., Jeffery A. Lepine, Nathan P. Podsakoff, and Jessica Siegel Christian. 2016. "Are Workplace Friendships a Mixed Blessing? Exploring Tradeoffs of Multiplex Relationships and Their Associations with Job Performance." *Personnel Psychology* 69, no. 2 (April): 311–55.

Miller, Carol T., and Cheryl R. Kaiser. 2001. "A Theoretical Perspective on Coping with Stigma." *Journal of Social Issues* 57, no. 1 (Spring): 73–92.

Minority Corporate Counsel Association (MCCA). 2021. "MCCA Law Firm Diversity Survey 2021." https://www.mcca.com/wp-content/uploads/2021/12/2021-MCCA-Law-Firm-Diversity-Survey-Report.pdf.

Mohler, John. 2017. "Cognac's Ethnic Division in the US—Focus." *Just Drinks,* January 6. https://www.just-drinks.com/features/cognacs-ethnic-division-in-the-us-focus/.

Moore, Wendy Leo. 2008. *Reproducing Racism: White Space, Elite Law Schools, and Racial Inequality.* Lanham, MD: Rowman & Littlefield.

———. 2020. "The Mechanisms of White Space(s)." *American Behavioral Scientist* 64, no. 14 (December): 1946–60.

Morgan Stanley. 2021. *2021 Diversity and Inclusion Report.* https://www.morganstanley.com/assets/pdfs/2021-diversity-and-inclusion-report.pdf.

Morrissey, Tracie Egan. 2019. "When Will a Reckoning on Racism Catch Up with Reality TV?" *New York Times,* October 29, 2019. https://www.nytimes.com/2019/10/29/style/bravo-real-housewives-race.html.

Mouw, Ted, and Barbara Entwisle. 2006. "Residential Segregation and Interracial Friendship in Schools." *American Journal of Sociology* 112, no. 2 (September): 394–441.

Mullainathan, Sendhil, and Eldar Shafir. 2013. *Scarcity: The New Science of Having Less and How It Defines Our Lives.* New York: Picador Books.

Murrell, Audrey J., Stacy Blake-Beard, and David M. Porter Jr. 2021. "The Importance of Peer Mentoring, Identity Work and Holding Environments: A Study of African American Leadership Development." *International Journal of Environmental Research and Public Health* 18, no. 9: 4920.

National Association for Law Placement (NALP). 2019. "Representation of Women and Minority Equity Partners among Partners Little Changed in Recent Years." *NALP Bulletin.* April. https://www.nalp.org/0419research.

NBC News. 2014. "Wall Street Fights to Keep Young, Restless Analysts." Markets, February 19, 2014. https://www.nbcnews.com/business/markets/wall-street-fights-keep-young-restless-analysts-n33641.

Neckerman, Kathryn M., Prudence L. Carter, and Jennifer C. Lee. 1999. "Segmented Assimilation and Minority Cultures of Mobility." *Ethnic and Racial Studies* 22, no. 6 (November): 945–65.

Neely, Megan Tobias. 2018. "Fit to Be King: How Patrimonialism on Wall Street Leads to Inequality." *Socio-Economic Review* 16, no. 2 (April): 365–85.

Nelson, Robert L. 1988. *Partners with Power: The Social Transformation of the Large Law Firm.* Berkeley: University of California Press.

Nelson, Robert L., Ioana Sendroiu, Ronit Dinovitzer, and Meghan Dawe.

2019. "Perceiving Discrimination: Race, Gender, and Sexual Orientation in the Legal Workplace." *Law & Society Inquiry* 44, no. 4 (November): 1051–82.

Niemann, Yolanda Flores, and John F. Dovidio. 1998. "Relationship of Solo Status, Academic Rank, and Perceived Distinctiveness to Job Satisfaction of Racial/Ethnic Minorities." *Journal of Applied Psychology* 83, no. 1 (February): 55–71.

O'Brien, Laurie T., and Brenda Major. 2005. "System-Justifying Beliefs and Psychological Well-Being: The Roles of Group Status and Identity." *Personality and Social Psychology Bulletin* 31, no. 12 (December): 1718–29.

O'Connell, Michael. 2014. "Race and Reality: The Quiet Success of the Black Unscripted Boom." *Hollywood Reporter*, April 3, 2014.

O'Donnell, Jayne. 2006. "Should Business Execs Meet at Strip Clubs?" *USA Today*, March 22, 2006. https://usatoday30.usatoday.com/money/companies/management/2006-03-22-strip-clubs-usat_x.htm.

Olson, Elizabeth. 2021. "In the World of Big Law Dealmaking, Black Lawyers Are Scarce." *Bloomberg Law*, July 15, 2021. https://news.bloomberglaw.com/business-and-practice/in-the-world-of-big-law-dealmaking-black-lawyers-are-scarce.

Oltmann, S. 2016. "Qualitative Interviews: A Methodological Discussion of the Interviewer and Respondent Contexts." *Forum: Qualitative Social Research* 17, no. 2 (May): 1–16.

Operario, Don, and Susan T. Fiske. 2001. "Ethnic Identity Moderates Perceptions of Prejudice: Judgments of Personal Versus Group Discrimination and Subtle Versus Blatant Bias." *Personality and Social Psychology Bulletin* 27, no. 5 (May): 550–61.

Orfield, Gary, John Kucsera, and Genevieve Siegel-Hawley. 2012. "E Pluribus . . . Separation: Deepening Double Segregation for More Students." *Civil Rights Project* (September): 1–96.

Orom, Heather, Chaman Sharma, Gregory G. Homish, Willie Underwood III, and D. Lynn Homish. 2017. "Racial Discrimination and Stigma Consciousness Are Associated with Higher Blood Pressure and Hypertension in Minority Men." *Journal of Racial and Ethnic Health Disparities* 4, no. 5 (October): 819–26.

Osborne, Danny, Nikhil K. Sengupta, and Chris G. Sibley. 2019. "System Justification theory at 25: Evaluating a Paradigm Shift in Psychology and Looking towards the Future." *British Journal of Social Psychology* 58, no. 2 (April): 340–61. https://doi.org/10.1111/bjso.12302.

Owuamalam, Chuma Kevin, Mark Rubin, and Russell Spears. 2019. "Revisiting 25 Years of System Motivation Explanation for System Justification from the Perspective of Social Identity Model of System Attitudes." *British Journal of Social Psychology* 58, no. 2 (April): 362–81.

Page-Gould, Elizabeth, Rodolfo Mendoza-Denton, and Wendy Berry Mendes. 2014. "Stress and Coping in Interracial Contexts: The Influence of Race-Based Rejection Sensitivity and Cross-Group Friendship in Daily Experiences of Health." *Journal of Social Issues* 70, no. 2 (June): 256–78.

Pager, Devah. 2007. *Marked: Race, Crime, and Finding Work in an Era of Mass Incarceration.* Chicago: University of Chicago Press.

Pager, Devah, and Hana Shephard. 2008. "The Sociology of Discrimination: Racial Discrimination in Employment, Housing, Credit, and Consumer Markets." *Annual Review of Sociology* 34 (August): 181–209.

Pan, J. C. 2020. "Why Diversity Training Isn't Enough." *New Republic,* January 7, 2020. https://newrepublic.com/article/156032/diversity -training-isnt-enough-pamela-newkirk-robin-diangelo-books-reviews.

Pao, Ellen K. 2017. *Reset: My Fight for Inclusion and Lasting Change.* New York: Spiegel & Grau.

Pascoe, Elizabeth A., and Laura Smart Richman. 2009. "Perceived Discrimination and Health: A Meta-analytic Review." *Psychological Bulletin* 135, no. 4 (July): 531–54.

Patterson, Orlando. 2014. "Making Sense of Culture." *Annual Review of Sociology* 40, no. 1 (July): 1–30.

Patrice, Joe. 2020. "Davis Polk Is Named after a Segregationist. . . . Perhaps It's Time to Consider a New Name." *Above the Law,* June 17, 2020. https://abovethelaw.com/2020/06/davis-polk-is-named-after-a -segregationist-perhaps-its-time-to-consider-a-new-name/?amp=1.

Payne-Pikus, Monique R., John Hagan, and Robert L. Nelson. 2010. "Experiencing Discrimination: Race and Retention in America's Largest Law Firms." *Law & Society Review* 44, nos. 3/4 (September/December): 553–84.

Pearce, Russell G. 2005. "White Lawyering: Rethinking Race, Lawyer Identity, and Rule of Law." *Fordham Law Review* 73, no. 5 (April): 2081–99.

Phillips, Katherine W., Tracy L. Dumas, and Nancy P. Rothbard. 2018. "Diversity and Authenticity." *Harvard Business Review* (March–April). https://hbr.org/2018/03/diversity-and-authenticity.

Piazza, Jo. 2018. "The Quiet Efforts to Battle Silicon Valley's Bro Culture."

Wall Street Journal, November 11, 2018. https://www.wsj.com/articles/the-quiet-efforts-to-battle-silicon-valleys-bro-culture-1541943938.

Pinel, Elizabeth C. 1999. "Stigma Consciousness: The Psychological Legacy of Social Stereotypes." *Journal of Personality and Social Psychology* 76, no. 1 (January): 114–28.

———. 2004. "You're Just Saying That Because I'm a Woman: Stigma Consciousness and Attributions to Discrimination." *Self and Identity* 3, no. 1: 39–51.

Pinel, Elizabeth C., Leah R. Warner, and Poh-Pheng Chua. 2005. "Getting There Is Only Half the Battle: Stigma Consciousness and Maintaining Diversity." *Journal of Social Issues* 61, no. 3 (August): 481–506.

Plant, E. Ashby, and Patricia G. Devine. 2003. "The Antecedents and Implications of Interracial Anxiety." *Personality and Social Psychology Bulletin* 29, no. 6 (June): 790–801.

Portes, Alejandro, and Min Zhou. 1993. "The New Second Generation: Segmented Assimilation and Its Variants among Post-1965 Immigrant Youth." *ANNALS of the American Academy of Political and Social Science* 530, no. 1 (November): 74–96.

Prichep. 2013. "A Campus More Diverse than Reality: Beware That Campus Brochure." *NPR*, December 29, 2013. https://www.npr.org/2013/12/29/257765543/a-campus-more-colorful-than-reality-beware-that-college-brochure.

Purcell, David. 2013. "Baseball, Beer, and Bulgari: Examining Cultural Capital and Gender Inequality in a Retail Fashion Corporation." *Journal of Contemporary Ethnography* 42, no. 3 (June): 291–319.

Purdie-Vaughns, Valerie, Claude M. Steele, Paul G. Davies, Ruth Ditlmann, and Jennifer Randall Crosby. 2008. "Social Identity Contingencies: How Diversity Cues Signal Threat or Safety for African Americans in Mainstream Institutions." *Journal of Personality and Social Psychology* 94, no. 4 (April): 615–30.

Quillian, Lincoln. 2006. "New Approaches to Understanding Racial Prejudice and Discrimination." *Annual Review of Sociology* 32 (August): 299–328.

Quillian, Lincoln, Devah Pager, Ole Hexel, and Arnfinn H. Midtbøen. 2017. "Meta-analysis of Field Experiments Shows No Change in Racial Discrimination in Hiring over Time." *PNAS* 114, no. 41 (October): 10870–75.

Ramsey, Donovan X. 2015. "The Truth about Black Twitter." *Atlantic*,

April 10, 2015. https://www.theatlantic.com/technology/archive/2015/ 04/the-truth-about-black-twitter/390120/.

Ray, Victor. 2019. "A Theory of Racialized Organizations." *American Sociological Review* 84, no. 1 (February): 26–53.

Reardon, Sean F. 2016. "School Segregation and Racial Academic Achievement Gaps." *Russell Sage Foundation Journal of the Social Sciences* 2, no. 5 (September): 34–57.

Reeves, Arin N. 2014. "Written in Black & White: Exploring Confirmation Bias in Racialized Perceptions of Writing Skills." Yellow Paper Series. Nextions. http://diversity.missouristate.edu/assets/ diversityconference/14468226472014040114WritteninBlackand WhitevYPS.pdf.

Reeves, Richard V. 2017. *Dream Hoarders: How the American Upper Middle Class Is Leaving Everyone Else in the Dust, Why That Is a Problem, and What to Do about It.* Washington, DC: Brookings Institution Press.

Rich, Camille Gear. 2004. "Performing Racial and Ethnic Identity: Discrimination by Proxy and the Future of Title VII." *New York University Law Review* 79, no. 4 (October): 1134–1270.

Ridgeway, Cecilia L. 2019. *Status: Why Is It Everywhere? Why Does it Matter?* New York: Russell Sage Foundation.

Rigney, Daniel. 2010. *The Matthew Effect: How Advantage Begets Further Advantage.* New York: Columbia University Press.

Rivera, Lauren A. 2012. "Hiring as Cultural Matching: The Case of Elite Professional Service Firms." *American Sociological Review* 77, no. 6 (December): 999–1022.

———. 2015. *Pedigree: How Elite Students Get Elite Jobs.* Princeton, NJ: Princeton University Press.

Roberts, Laura Morgan. 2005. "Changing Faces: Professional Image Construction in Diverse Organizational Settings." *Academy of Management Review* 30, no. 4 (October): 685–711.

Root, Veronica. 2014. "Retaining Color." *University of Michigan Journal of Law Reform* 47, no. 3 (April): 575–643.

Roscigno, Vincent J., Lisette M. Garcia, and Donna Bobbitt-Zeher. 2007. "Social Closure and Processes of Race/Sex Employment Discrimination." *ANNALS of the American Academy of Political and Social Science* 609, no. 1 (January): 16–48.

Ross, Lawrence. 2016. *Blackballed: The Black and White Politics of Race on America's Campuses.* New York: St. Martin's Press.

Rothstein, Richard. 2017. *The Color of Law: A Forgotten History of How Our Government Segregated America*. New York: Liveright.

Sander, Richard H. 2006. "The Racial Paradox of the Corporate Law Firm." *North Carolina Law Review* 84, no. 5 (June): 1755–1822.

Scheiber, Noam, and John Eligon. 2019. "Elite Law Firm's All-White Partner Class Stirs Debate on Diversity." *New York Times*, January 27, 2019. https://www.nytimes.com/2019/01/27/us/paul-weiss-partner-diversity-law-firm.html.

Schmitt, Kellie. 2006. "Corporate Diversity Demands Put Pressure on Outside Counsel." *ALM Media News*, December 28, 2006. https://www.law.com/corpcounsel/almID/1167214010196.

Seibert, Scott E., Maria L. Kraimer, and Robert C. Liden. 2001. "A Social Capital Theory of Career Success." *Academy of Management Journal* 44, no. 2 (April): 219–37.

Sellers, Robert M., and J. Nicole Shelton. 2003. "The Role of Racial Identity in Perceived Racial Discrimination." *Journal of Personality and Social Psychology* 84, no. 5 (May): 1079–92.

Shepperd, James, Wendi Malone, and Kate Sweeny. 2008. "Exploring Causes of the Self-Serving Bias." *Social and Personality Psychology Compass* 2, no. 2 (March): 895–908.

Simmons, Christine. 2019. "170 GCs Pen Open Letter to Law Firms: Improve on Diversity or Lose Our Business." *American Lawyer*, January 27, 2019. https://www.law.com/americanlawyer/2019/01/27/170-gcs-pen-open-letter-to-law-firms-improve-on-diversity-or-lose-our-business/.

Sloan, Melissa M., Ranae J. Evenson Newhouse, and Ashley B. Thompson. 2013. "Counting on Coworkers: Race, Social Support, and Emotional Experiences on the Job." *Social Psychology Quarterly* 76, no. 4 (December): 343–72.

Small, Mario Luis, David J. Harding, and Michèle Lamont. 2010. "Reconsidering Culture and Poverty." *ANNALS of the American Academy of Political and Social Science* 629, no. 1 (May): 6–27.

Smith, Patrick. 2020. "8 Firms Have Announced High-Level Diversity Positions in the Last Month. How Should We Feel about That?" *American Lawyer*, November 12, 2020. https://www.law.com/americanlawyer/2020/11/12/eight-firms-have-announced-high-level-diversity-positions-in-the-last-month-how-should-we-feel-about-that/.

Spencer, Steven J., Christine Logel, and Paul G. Davies. 2016. "Stereotype Threat." *Annual Review of Psychology* 67 (January): 415–37.

Spiezio, Caroline. 2020a. "A Year after General Counsel Letter Pushed for Diversity, Slow Change." Reuters, February 6. https://www.reuters .com/article/usa-lawyer-general-counsel-diversity/a-year-after-general -counsel-letter-pushed-for-diversity-slow-change-idUSL1N2A6oFI.

———. 2020b. "Microsoft Raises Rewards for Outside Law Firms That Promote Black and Latino Lawyers." Reuters, September 30. https:// www.reuters.com/article/lawyer-diversity-microsoft/microsoft-raises -reward-for-outside-law-firms-that-promote-black-and-latino-lawyers -idUSL1N2GR1LH.

Stearns, Elizabeth, Claudia Buchmann, and Kara Bonneau. 2009. "Interracial Friendships in the Transition to College: Do Birds of a Feather Flock To- gether Once They Leave the Nest?" *Sociology of Education* 82, no. 2: 173–95.

Steele, Claude M., and Joshua M. Aronson. 1995. "Stereotype Threat and the Intellectual Test Performance of African-Americans." *Journal of Personality and Social Psychology* 69, no. 5 (December): 797–811.

Stephan, Walter G. 2014. "Intergroup Anxiety: Theory, Research, and Prac- tice." *Personality and Social Psychology Review* 18, no. 3 (August): 239–55.

Stephens, Neil. 2007. "Collecting Data from Elites and Ultra Elites: Tele- phone and Face-to-Face Interviews with Microeconomists." *Qualitative Research* 7, no. 2: 203–16. https://doi.org/10.1177/1468794107076020.

Stroebe, Katherine, John F. Dovidio, Manuela Barreto, Naomi Ellemers, and Melissa-Sue John. 2010. "Is the World a Just Place? Countering the Negative Consequences of Pervasive Discrimination by Affirming the World as Just." *British Journal of Social Psychology* 50, no. 3 (Septem- ber): 484–500.

Sturges, Judith E., and Kathleen J. Hanrahan. 2004. "Comparing Tele- phone and Face-to-Face Qualitative Interviewing: A Research Note." *Qualitative Research* 4, no. 1: 107–18.

Sturm, Susan. 2001. "Second Generation Employment Discrimination: A Structural Approach." *Columbia Law Review* 101, no. 3 (April): 458–568.

Swencionis, Jillian K., Cydney H. Dupree, and Susan T. Fiske. 2017. "Warmth-Competence Tradeoffs in Impression Management Across Race and Social-Class Divides." *Journal of Social Issues* 73, no. 1 (March): 175–91.

Tansey, Oisín. 2007. "Process Tracing and Elite Interviewing: A Case for

Non-probability Sampling." *PS: Political Science and Politics* 40, no. 4 (October): 765–72.

Tatum, Beverly Daniel. 2017. *Why Are All the Black Kids Sitting Together in the Cafeteria? And Other Conversations about Race*. New York: Basic Books.

Taylor, Evi, Patricia Guy-Walls, Patricia Wilkerson, and Rejoice Addae. 2019. "The Historical Perspectives of Stereotypes on African-American Males." *Journal of Human Rights and Social Work* 4, no. 3: 213–25.

Thiem, Kelsey C., Rebecca Neel, Austin J. Simpson, and Andrew R. Todd. 2019. "Are Black Women and Girls Associated with Danger? Implicit Racial Bias at the Intersection of Target Age and Gender." *Personality and Social Psychology Bulletin* 45, no. 10 (October): 1427–39.

Thomas, David A., and John J. Gabarro. 1999. *Breaking Through: The Making of Minority Executives in Corporate America*. Boston: Harvard Business School Press.

Thompson, Derek. 2014. "Which Sports Have the Whitest/Richest/ Oldest Fans?" *Atlantic*, February 10, 2014. https://www.theatlantic .com/business/archive/2014/02/which-sports-have-the-whitest -richest-oldest-fans/283626/.

Thompson, Mischa, and Denise Sekaquaptewa. 2002. "When Being Different Is Detrimental: Solo Status and the Performance of Women and Racial Minorities." *Analyses of Social Issues and Public Policy* 2, no. 1 (December): 183–203.

Thompson, Phillip S., and Mark C. Bolino. 2018. "Negative Beliefs about Accepting Coworker Help: Implications for Employee Attitudes, Job Performance, and Reputation." *Journal of Applied Psychology* 103, no. 8 (August): 842–66.

Tilly, Charles. 1998. *Durable Inequality*. Berkeley: University of California Press.

Tippett, Elizabeth. 2012. "Robbing a Barren Vault: The Implications of Dukes v. Wal-Mart for Cases Challenging Subjective Employment Practices." *Hofstra Labor and Employment Law Journal* 29, no. 2: 433–83.

———. 2019. "Opportunity Discrimination: A Hidden Liability Employers Can Fix." *Employee Rights and Employment Policy Journal* 23, no. 1: 165–97.

Torres, Kimberly C., and Camille Z. Charles. 2004. "Metastereotypes and the Black-White Divide: A Qualitative View of Race on an Elite College Campus." *Du Bois Review* 1, no. 1 (March): 115–49.

Travis, Dnika, J., Jennifer Thorpe-Moscon, and Courtney McCluney. 2016. *Emotional Tax: How Black Women and Men Pay More at Work and How Leaders Can Take Action (Report)*. Catalyst, October 11. https://www.catalyst.org/research/emotional-tax-how-black-women-and-men-pay-more-at-work-and-how-leaders-can-take-action/.

Trawalter, Sophie, Jennifer A. Richeson, and J. Nicole Shelton. 2009. "Predicting Behavior During Interracial Interactions: A Stress and Coping Approach." *Personality and Social Psychology Review* 13, no. 4: 243–68.

Turco, Catherine J. 2010. "Cultural Foundations of Tokenism: Evidence from the Leveraged Buyout Industry." *American Sociological Review* 75, no. 6 (December): 894–913.

Turner, Ralph, H. 1960. "Sponsored and Contest Mobility and the School System." *American Sociological Review* 25, no. 6 (December): 855–62. https://doi.org/10.2307/2089982.

Tyler, Imogen. 2020. *Stigma: The Machinery of Inequality*. London: Zed Books.

Tyson, Karolyn. 2011. *Integration Interrupted: Tracking, Black Students, and Acting White after Brown*. Oxford: Oxford University Press.

US Commission on Civil Rights. 2018. *Public Education Funding Inequity in an Era of Increasing Concentration of Poverty and Resegregation*. Washington, DC. https://www.usccr.gov/pubs/2018/2018-01-10-Education-Inequity.pdf.

US Department of the Interior, US Fish and Wildlife Service, and US Department of Commerce, US Census Bureau. 2016. *2016 National Survey of Fishing, Hunting, and Wildlife-Associated Recreation*. US Fish and Wildlife Service, US Department of Commerce, and US Census Bureau. https://www.fws.gov/wsfrprograms/subpages/nationalsurvey/nat_survey2016.pdf.

Viator, Ralph E. 2001. "An Examination of African Americans' Access to Public Accounting Mentors: Perceived Barriers and Intentions to Leave." *Accounting, Organizations and Society* 26, no. 6 (August): 541–61.

Vogl, Susanne. 2013. "Telephone versus Face-to-Face Interviews: Mode Effect on Semistructured Interviews with Children." *Sociological Methodology* 43, no. 1 (September): 133–77.

Wald, Eli. 2009. "Glass Ceilings and Dead Ends: Professional Ideologies: Gender Stereotypes, and the Future of Women Lawyers at Large Law Firms." *Fordham Law Review* 78, no. 5: 2245–88.

Wang, Katie, Katherine Stroebe, and John F. Dovidio. 2012. "Stigma Consciousness and Prejudice Ambiguity: Can It Be Adaptive to Perceive the World as Biased?" *Personality and Individual Differences* 53, no. 3 (August): 241–45.

Wengraf, Tom. 2001. *Qualitative Research Interviewing: Biographic Narrative and Semi-Structured Methods.* London: SAGE Publications.

Weiss, Suzannah. 2016. "The Huggle App Matches You Based on Where You Like to Go—Not on Your Appearance." *Bustle*, August 17, 2016. https://www.bustle.com/articles/175495-the-huggle-app-matches-you -based-on-where-you-like-to-go-not-on-your.

Wilder, Gita Z. 2008. "Race and Ethnicity in the Legal Profession: Findings from the First Wave of the After the JD Study—An After the JD Monograph." The NALP Foundation for Law Career Research and Education and the National Association for Law Placement, Inc. (NALP). http://www.nalp.org/assets/1064_ajdraceethnicity monograph.pdf.

Wilkins, David B., and G. Mitu Gulati. 1996. "Why Are There So Few Black Lawyers in Corporate Law Firms—An Institutional Analysis." *California Law Review* 84, no. 3 (May): 493–625.

———. 1998. "Reconceiving the Tournament of Lawyers: Tracking, Seeding, and Information Control in Elite Law Firms." *Virginia Law Review* 84, no. 8 (November): 1581–1681.

Williams, Christine L., Chandra Muller, and Kristine Kilanski. 2012. "Gendered Organizations in the New Economy." *Gender & Society* 26, no. 4 (August): 549–73.

Williams, Thomas Chatterton. 2011. *Losing My Cool: Love, Literature, and a Black Man's Escape from the Crowd.* New York: Penguin.

Wilson, George, Ian Sakura-Lemessy, and Jonathan P. West. 1999. "Reaching the Top: Racial Differences in Mobility Paths to Upper-Tier Occupations." *Work and Occupations* 26, no. 2 (May): 165–86.

Wilson, William Julius. 1987. *The Truly Disadvantaged: The Inner City, the Underclass, and Public Policy.* Chicago: University of Chicago Press.

Wingfield, Adia Harvey. 2010. "Are Some Emotions Marked 'Whites Only'? Racialized Feelings Rules in Professional Workplaces." *Social Problems* 57, no. 2 (May): 251–68.

———. 2012. *No More Invisible Man: Race and Gender in Men's Work.* Philadelphia: Temple University Press.

———. 2014. "Crossing the Color Line: Black Professional Men's Development of Interracial Social Networks." *Societies* 4, no. 2 (May): 240–55.

———. 2019. *Flatlining: Race, Work, and Healthcare in the New Economy.* Oakland: University of California Press.

Woodson, Kevin. 2015. "Race and Rapport: Homophily and Racial Disadvantage in Large Law Firms." *Fordham Law Review* 83 (5): 2557–76.

———. 2016a. "Derivative Racial Discrimination." *Stanford Journal of Civil Rights & Civil Liberties* 12, no. 2 (June): 335–87.

———. 2016b. "Diversity without Integration." *Penn State Law Review* 120 (3): 807–66.

———. 2016c. "Human Capital Discrimination, Law Firm Inequality, and the Limits of Title VII." *Cardozo Law Review* 38 (1): 183–229.

Yates, Clinton. 2012. "I'm a Black Hockey Fan: We Do Exist." *Washington Post*, March 2, 2012. https://www.washingtonpost.com/opinions/im-a-black-hockey-fan-we-do-exist/2012/02/27/gIQAa7MHnR_story.html.

Yoshino, Kenji. 2006. *Covering: The Hidden Assault on Our Civil Rights.* New York: Random House.

Yuracko, Kimberly A. 2006. "Trait Discrimination as Race Discrimination: An Argument about Assimilation." *George Washington Law Review* 74, no. 3 (April): 365–438.

Zelevansky, Nora. 2019. "The Big Business of Unconscious Bias." *New York Times*, November 20, 2019. https://www.nytimes.com/2019/11/20/style/diversity-consultants.html.

Zraick, Karen. 2018. "Lawyers Say They Face Persistent Racial and Gender Bias at Work." *New York Times*, September 6, 2018. https://www.nytimes.com/2018/09/06/us/lawyers-bias-racial-gender.html.

Index

alcohol, 18; beer, 80, 83, 88, 95–96; drinking sessions at White bars, 96; happy hours, 72; workplace banter and camaraderie, 81

Armstrong, Elizabeth, 96

Asian workers, 145

assignments, 24; discrepancies in, 21–23, 27–29; "grabbing," 25; grunt work, 23; paper work, 23; preferential access to, 27; second-order effects, 28

authenticity, 65

Bain & Co., 18

Black Americans, 66, 76–77, 144; Black racial identity, negative stereotypes and prejudices, 46–47; Black social spheres, 81; interracial immersion, limited opportunities for, 116, 117; stigma anxiety, 47; White people, limited prior social relationships with, 90

Black ceiling, 4, 12, 16

Blackness, 45, 108

Black-owned firms, 143–44

Black professionals, 171–72n7, 172n17; adaptive responses, 45–46, 67; alienation of, 3, 80, 81, 82–83, 99; Black ceiling, 16; burning out, 29; career capital, 105, 109–10; career capital, limiting access to, 67; chance, role of, 102, 104–6; "change who they are," pressure to, 80; class-based differences, 3, 96–99; comfort interacting with White people, 105–7; confirmation bias, 49; coping and defensive mechanisms, 45, 66–67; criticism from other Black professionals, 63–67; cultural alienation and racial bias, 85–86, 96; cultural capital, 68–69, 76, 86–87, 97, 138; cultural differences, 73–74, 78, 79; cultural difficulties of, 3;

cultural homophily, 111–12; discretionary relationships, 38–40; discrimination, risk of, 3, 51–52, 55, 58, 63, 67, 103, 129–30, 134; discriminatory punitiveness, risk of, 50; at elite firms, 3–4, 17–19, 45, 101, 117, 121, 124, 126, 130–31, 144–45, 153–56, 160; fear of being "angry Black person," 58–59; fear of being judged incompetent, 55–58; fear of seeming threatening, 59–60; homophily preferences, 11; human capital, development of, 132–33; institutional discrimination, 15, 43; integrated personal backgrounds, 11–12; interactional ease, in White social spaces, 105–11; interracial friendships, as limited, 89–90; interracial interactions, 116, 124, 142–43; interviews of, 156–58; isolation of, 3, 82; mentorship, 8, 40, 97, 102, 104, 106, 122, 131–32, 136, 139; microaggressions, 93, 123; as outcasts/outsiders, 3, 82, 84, 99, 126; partnership-level positions, 101–2, 106; performance reviews, subjectivity of, 33–35; personal information, avoidance of sharing, 45; pop culture references, as unfamiliar, 78; race, significance of, 118–23, 153, 159–60; racial bias, 2–3, 48–49, 52, 68, 83, 85, 100, 126, 130, 145; racial disadvantage, 4, 13, 21, 25–26, 47, 99–100, 120, 124–27, 153, 158, 160; racial discomfort, 16, 124, 126–29, 130–31, 133, 137–38, 144, 172n22; racial discomfort, and implicit bias, 134–35; racial discrimination, 83, 85; racial disparities, 48–49; racial isolation, 54, 120; racial patterns, in tastes and interests, 75–76; racial reticence, 47, 55–58, 64, 66–67; racial risk management, 5–6, 45–46, 52, 67; racial separateness, 11; racial stress,